T0334320

Cambridge Elements ≡

Elements in Politics and Society in Southeast Asia
edited by
Edward Aspinall
Australian National University
Meredith L. Weiss
University at Albany, SUNY

STATE AND SUB-STATE NATIONALISM IN SOUTHEAST ASIA

Jacques Bertrand
University of Toronto

CAMBRIDGE
UNIVERSITY PRESS

Shaftesbury Road, Cambridge CB2 8EA, United Kingdom

One Liberty Plaza, 20th Floor, New York, NY 10006, USA

477 Williamstown Road, Port Melbourne, VIC 3207, Australia

314–321, 3rd Floor, Plot 3, Splendor Forum, Jasola District Centre, New Delhi – 110025, India

103 Penang Road, #05–06/07, Visioncrest Commercial, Singapore 238467

Cambridge University Press is part of Cambridge University Press & Assessment, a department of the University of Cambridge.

We share the University's mission to contribute to society through the pursuit of education, learning and research at the highest international levels of excellence.

www.cambridge.org
Information on this title: www.cambridge.org/9781009583060

DOI: 10.1017/9781009583046

First published 2024

A catalogue record for this publication is available from the British Library

ISBN 978-1-009-58306-0 Hardback
ISBN 978-1-009-58303-9 Paperback
ISSN 2515-2998 (online)
ISSN 2515-298X (print)

State and Sub-state Nationalism in Southeast Asia

Elements in Politics and Society in Southeast Asia

DOI: 10.1017/9781009583046
First published online: December 2024

Jacques Bertrand
University of Toronto

Author for correspondence: Jacques Bertrand, jacques.bertrand@utoronto.ca

Abstract: Nationalism is a political phenomenon with deep roots in Southeast Asia. Yet, state attempts to create homogenous nations met with resistance. This Element focuses on understanding the rise and subsequent ebbing of sub-state nationalist mobilization in response to state nationalism. Two factors allowed sub-state nationalist movements to be formed and persist: first, state nationalisms that were insufficiently inclusive; second, the state's use of authoritarian tools to implement its nationalist agenda. But Southeast Asian states were able to reduce sub-state nationalist mobilization when they changed their policies to meet two conditions: i) some degree of explicit recognition of the distinctiveness of groups; ii) institutional flexibility toward regional/local territorial units to accommodate a high degree of group self-governance. The Element focuses on four states in the region – namely Indonesia, the Philippines, Thailand, and Myanmar.

Keywords: East Asian politics and society, Asian studies, international relations, political economy, comparative politics

ISBNs: 9781009583060 (HB), 9781009583039 (PB), 9781009583046 (OC)
ISSNs: 2515-2998 (online), 2515-298X (print)

Contents

Introduction

Nationalism is a political phenomenon with deep roots in Southeast Asia. As scholars of nationalism broadly agree, it emerged mostly as a product of modern capitalism and increasing scale of territorial expansion. In Southeast Asia, anti-colonial nationalist movements were strong, and they mixed with an array of mobilizational forms from revolutions to communist resistance. As elsewhere, nationalists aspired to carve new states out of colonial empires or, once states were formed, to foster unity of their newly freed peoples. The "nation," as a modern, equalizing and, in principle, unifying form of identity was a new tool for post-independence state leaders who aspired to both eliminate remnants of colonial hierarchies and create new, modern modes of governance rather than return to any real or imagined pre-colonial form. In doing so, they also sought to eliminate many of the internal differences that they perceived as obstacles to the unity, both of state and nation, that the Westphalian state system elevated as the twentieth-century's model of equality and sovereignty.

Yet, these homogenizing attempts to create single nations coinciding with post-colonial states met with strong resistance. Several groups developed alternative nationalisms, to contest post-independence state boundaries and secure their own states. They developed their own aspirations to sovereignty and sought recognition for their respective nations. These alternative, sub-state nationalisms clashed significantly with state leaders' attempts to craft single nations within their borders. Why has Southeast Asia seen many of these alternative nationalisms arise and persist over several decades after independence? Why were some of these nationalist movements able eventually to accept existing state boundaries, and exist peacefully alongside the dominant state nationalism they previously rejected?

This Element is primarily focused on understanding the rise and subsequent ebbing of sub-state nationalist mobilization, in a region where state nationalism was strong. Ethnic, cultural, and religious diversity is not only very high across the region, but within state boundaries as well. The classic, and probably most cited work on nationalism, Benedict Anderson's *Imagined Communities,* drew strong inspiration from Southeast Asian nationalist movements that rose during colonial rule and eventually claimed independence for their respective nations. These movements managed to build new identities as nations that superseded ethnic, cultural, and religious differences. As Anderson also observed in the region and more broadly, nationalism became a powerful tool for state leaders to create unity, including in new post-colonial independent states.

In some cases, however, alternative nationalisms contested the new nations that these movements created and that became institutionalized in newly independent states. Acehnese, Papuans, Moros, Malay Muslims, Karen, and many others developed sub-state nationalisms, by which I mean they developed an identity as nations aspiring to carve a state out of the existing one in which they resided. None of these groups were nations in any objective sense. That they developed sub-state nationalist movements was not inevitable and predicated on any essentialist conception of nation. As I discuss below, nations are constructed and are shaped both by particular circumstances as well as leadership. Ethnic, cultural, and even religious identities can sometimes provide some of the material upon which nationalists construct an identity as a nation, but these are neither necessary nor inevitably nationalist in orientation.

I divide the analysis into two parts. First, I focus on the question of the formation of sub-state nationalist groups and movements in the region. Second, I briefly discuss why some of these movements, once mobilized, were able to accept and adhere to existing state boundaries.

There are few, if any factors that can explain the rise and intensification of *all* sub-state nationalisms in Southeast Asia. Yet, a close comparison of small subsets helps to identify some common ones. My main argument is that two factors combined to make sub-state nationalist movements particularly likely to be formed and to persist: first, state nationalisms that were insufficiently inclusive and based on more narrowly defined shared identities tended to make some groups particularly excluded or marginalized; second, the state's use of authoritarian tools to intensify the implementation of its nationalist agenda against reluctant groups fueled the formation and/or solidification of sub-state nationalist responses.

Furthermore, there are several mediating factors that also contributed: i) a precondition was that groups are territorially concentrated; ii) groups that were administered separately from core groups during colonial rule were most likely to perceive state nationalism as exclusionary; iii) leadership is necessary to turn grievances and shape identities into national ones. Without nationalists, nations don't rise.

Once mobilized, sub-state nationalist movements do not easily subside, let alone disappear. Even though nations are constructed, and movement leadership shapes and channels group identities into nationalist ones, they don't easily reverse themselves and lose their nationalist aspirations. As nationalism is intrinsically tied to sovereignty, sub-state nationalist groups usually aim for their own state. Where they accept a compromise within existing state boundaries, it usually entails some degree of territorial autonomy and self-governance. I argue that Southeast Asian states were able to reduce sub-state nationalist mobilization when they changed their policies to meet two conditions: i) some degree of explicit recognition of the distinctiveness of groups; ii) institutional flexibility toward regional/local territorial units to accommodate a high degree of group self-governance. Accommodating only one dimension, although leading to periods of less tension, never produced lasting results. The region's diversity has required flexibility and imaginative accommodation in ways that have been incongruent with existing simplified, centralized, and mostly predatory state models.

I focus on four states in the region – namely Indonesia, the Philippines, Thailand, and Myanmar. These countries vary along a number of relevant factors. First, they have very different histories of colonialism and of anti-colonial movements. Thailand was never colonized, while all three others were subjected to different European colonial rulers. Indonesia and the Philippines lacked a history of strong pre-colonial state formation and political amalgamation under any dominant group, while Siam and Burma saw the rise of strong kingdoms whose influence spanned much of the area that current states occupy. Indonesia's anti-colonial movement had a revolutionary component, while the Philippines had an early revolutionary one that failed. In the end, both Burma and the Philippines obtained their independence progressively. Second, Indonesia, Thailand and Myanmar share histories of strong roles of their respective militaries in state governance, while the Philippines is the region's longest lasting democracy with only a brief period of strong authoritarian rule. Third, the structure of their original states varied considerably, with Thailand being a strongly centralized, unitary state; the Philippines adopting a US-style bicameral system with representation from provinces along non-ethnic lines; Indonesia with a centralized unitary state and originally without a chamber to represent its provinces; and Burma/Myanmar adopting constitutions that gave representation to regions (representing the Bamar majority) and several ethnic states.

Yet, within all four states significant sub-state nationalist movements arose. Acehnese, Papuans, Moros, Malay Muslims, Karen, Kachin, Chin, and other groups in Burma/Myanmar developed alternative identities as nations and political objectives of sovereignty. I trace the origins and formation of sub-state nationalist movements in each state, as well as their evolution. I identify the extent to which the expression and evolution of state nationalism over time, its degree of inclusiveness, and policies associated with it contributed to perceived group exclusion. In addition, I analyze the impact of attempts to repress or assimilate such groups.

I also discuss why, in two sub-state nationalist cases, groups found agreement with the state and accepted to remain within existing state boundaries and alongside the nation it claimed to represent. I show that Acehnese and Bangsamoro claims to self-determination were reduced once the Indonesian and Philippine states adapted state institutions to enshrine first, significant forms of group recognition and, second, governance powers over territories they claimed.

The Element does not address all possible or prior sub-state nationalist movements that appeared in the region. The preconditions set above, such as territorial concentration, leadership and, in some cases, areas that were administered separately under colonial rule certainly exclude a number of other groups. State nationalism in Indonesia for instance long marginalized ethnic Chinese who were too dispersed, too small, and with little nationalist leadership to develop an alternative sub-state nationalism. Many members of the Chinese diaspora more broadly in the region had adhered in the early twentieth century to Chinese nationalism, and organized movements that reflected events in China rather than directed to the society where they lived. But, as in the case of the Communist movement in Malaya, they had implications for how the Chinese would be integrated within the conception of state nationalism later. There was little opportunity to create bonds across ethnic barriers within Malaya, which would make the broader idea of a Malaysian nation ultimately fail to take root. Other groups, such as the Ambonese in the Republik Maluku Selatan (RMS) movement in 1950 quickly fizzled away, partly because the leadership of the movement, mostly arising from former KNIL soldiers of the Dutch colonial army, could not articulate a sub-state nationalist agenda that resonated broadly. Many Ambonese did not feel threatened and in fact adhered enthusiastically to the Indonesian Republic's idea of an Indonesian nation. It was certainly premature to think that state nationalism was not sufficiently inclusive in this case, and repression was targeted at the RMS movement and not against most Ambonese.

So, while the degree of inclusion of state nationalism and state repression are not predictors of all sub-state nationalist movements, they play significant roles in setting the base and fueling mobilization and support for sub-state nationalism. The focal analytical point draws attention to how an alternative idea of nation builds on the exclusion and repression that state nationalism creates.

Nationalism: Definition and Scope

Nationalism as a political phenomenon has been challenging to define and its ramifications difficult to analyze. In its original conceptualization, it was associated with some of the worst horrors of the twentieth century, in particular Nazi Germany's policy of Jewish extermination, but also conversely with the anti-colonial movement that inspired dozens of oppressed groups to reject colonial rule and aspire to self-determination. From the 1980s onwards, a vast interdisciplinary literature from historians to political scientists produced new ways of understanding this phenomenon, and sought to explain mostly its origins but also its spread.

In recent decades, the common reference to nationalism has branched out to include groups seeking to obtain independence and autonomy, and that mobilize along ethnic lines, but this literature has created a fair amount of conceptual confusion. Multiple forms of resistance to the state, or claims to identity differences, are commonly referred to as nationalist.. The degree to which culture, symbols, and ethnic traits form the basis of a nation certainly remains a core debate but nationalism retains its conceptual distinction mainly in its political objective of the quest for self-determination of the nation, whatever its core attributes might be (Hutchinson, 2004).

Ernest Gellner's classic definition is simple and remains relevant. Nationalism "is a political principle that holds that the political and the national unit should be congruent" (Gellner, 1983:1). As with other scholars of nationalism, Gellner made a clear distinction between the state and the nation. In a classic Weberian sense, the state is most often defined as a set of institutions whose "specific concern is with the organization of domination, in the name of the common interest, within a delimited territory." Territorial delimitation departs from other political organizations or proto-states, particularly in regions such as Southeast Asia, where borders were fluid for most centuries prior to the early twentieth (Day, 2002). The organization of domination in the common interest casts the state, in its modern form, as essentially representative of a people within this territory and with the institutional tools to govern. The "national unit" emerges from a people that, whether from bottom-up movements or elite-driven mobilization, come to see themselves as a nation.

The contribution of the literature on nationalism was to show that there was no natural, nor necessary, congruence between a people that defines itself as a "nation" and the state as a political unit. Individuals that found themselves enclosed within particular territorial boundaries did not necessarily identify with the institutions that governed them, nor was there any particular reason why the presence of such boundaries would create new bonds and feelings of belonging.

The "nation" therefore is distinct and not necessarily coincidental with the state. One of its most common definitions, and particularly relevant here, is Benedict Anderson's. As a Southeast Asianist, it is not surprising that his deep knowledge of the region inspired his definition of the nation as an "imagined political community" that is both "inherently limited and sovereign" (Anderson, 1991:5–6). The key elements of this definition pointed to the constructed nature of the political community, as not necessarily based on any preconceived, historically based characteristics, either ethnic or other. Furthermore, it can only be meaningful as limited in the sense that it distinguishes one political community from another. Comparison between inside and outside groups was an intrinsic part of delineating the community. While these characteristics might apply to a large number of political communities, the "inherently sovereign" is the defining feature of the nation. It implies that a political community seeks to govern itself, and therefore is intrinsically tied to self-determination.

Nationalism therefore is a political principle that implies active mobilization to define a nation and work toward its sovereignty. Nationalism can sometimes arise out of a grass-roots movement aspiring to self-determination. Groups that consider themselves as "nations" will aim to create congruence between state and nation, as the latter's sovereign aspiration is mainly realized, in the modern state system, when they have their own state.

But it might also mean that governing leaders will aim at congruence by attempting to create a nation from the people residing within state territorial boundaries. They do so with the expectation of fostering greater loyalty from their populations, and greater legitimacy for their rule. Anderson wrote of "official nationalism" to distinguish grass-roots national consciousness from the attempts by state leaders to use nationalism, as a modular form, to strengthen state legitimacy and sovereignty. These two forms of nationalism can occur independently from each other but, in some settings, might clash.

In both cases, the attributes of the nation can vary considerably, ranging from identifying a core ethnic trait as a base of inclusion and exclusion criteria for the nation, to a more inclusive allegiance based on political principles. Greenfeld made important distinctions between ethnic and civic forms that show why we cannot equate nationalism with an exclusionary agenda along ethnic (or racial) lines, nor necessarily with negative and violent agendas associated with some of its past expression in Nazi Germany or Eastern Europe. Rather the focus on "civic" forms points to the political character of the phenomenon, rather than its inherent association with ethnic characteristics. While the political agenda of self-determination, and creating a nation to coincide with state boundaries, sets the limits of the "nation," the glue that binds ranges from particular ethnic characteristics to sharing particular values (Greenfeld, 1992).

Why these varied forms arose is subject to many debates but two are particularly useful for understanding the Southeast Asian context. First, once it appeared, nationalism became, in Anderson's words, a "modular form" that could be replicated. State leaders found the example of rising nationalism in nineteenth-century Europe particularly compelling, especially how European leaders used vernacular languages as a base for building nations. Rulers adopted local vernaculars, elevated their status to provide a unique medium of communication, and reduced the use of multiple languages to build nations and reinvent the basis of legitimacy for their rule. Similar trends were observed in post-colonial contexts. Newly independent state leaders also copied the modular form of the nation and attempted to craft national identities to strengthen their legitimacy and rule.

Second, the character of the nations varied as states defined core elements as inherently distinct from others. They therefore required some form of identifier to mark this difference, but none were given or natural. While Anderson focused on language, other characteristics were sometimes equally, if not more, important. State leaders sometimes chose ethnic distinctions, religion, or cultural traits as core elements of their nation. When looking to build new states, notes Anthony Marx, elites reinforce the core nation by excluding some groups. He criticizes Anderson for missing the "central role of states in demarcating which particular community emerged and coincided with political institutions" (Marx, 2003:16). He further contends that "the emergence of nationalism can be explained according to the logic of exclusionary cohesion" (Marx, 2003:24). There are most often limits to any attempts for inclusion and a state imperative to exclude, sometimes brutally, certain groups to promote the homogeneity of the nation. Hechter called this phenomenon "state building nationalism" whereby state leaders seek to assimilate heterogenous populations into homogenous ones, with a goal of creating cultural homogeneity through inclusive or exclusive policies (Hechter, 2000:57–69). State nationalists therefore face a delicate balance between defining largely inclusive forms of nationalism to build loyalty and unity, yet requiring clear boundaries of the nation in order to do so. As a consequence, they often end up excluding groups within their boundaries.

While these two aspects of nationalism speak to its constructed nature, there are always limits to the malleability of the defined nation. State leaders select particular cultural characteristics, ethnic traits, or political values, and weave them into narratives that reconstruct histories and expand into state policies that consolidate and, to some extent, crystallize new nations. The insecurity of rule, the fragility of state boundaries, the thinness of legitimacy prompts state leaders to define and reify the nation, as a part of their toolkit of rule. A common vernacular language is one of several tools that states use to craft and unify these nations. The extent of cultural definition and markers of group boundaries can vary widely.

Once imposed, choices made could have deep implications for peripheral groups, which sometimes find a reason to mobilize along alternative nationalist lines. As Brubaker notes, the "nationalization of political space" has created "mutually antagonistic nationalisms," especially "nationalizing" nationalism in which claims are made "in the name of a 'core nation' or nationality, defined in ethnocultural terms, and sharply distinguished from the citizenry as a whole." It has also created "national minority nationalism" by which national minorities demand "state recognition of their distinct ethnocultural nationality, and the assertion of certain collective, nationality-based cultural or political rights" (Brubaker, 1996:4–6). Hechter offers a similar analysis in defining "peripheral nationalism" by which elites seek self-determination by separating from the host state. He notes that peripheral elites and masses attempt to maintain their identity and reduce incursions from the centre. They respond to the state that expands its reach and direct rule in areas where territories were typically under indirect rule but become increasingly powerless relative to the centre (Hechter, 2000:71). This tendency is particularly strong in response to state-building nationalism.

In sum, theories of nationalism have shown the strength and spread of the concept of the nation over the last century, while emphasizing its different expression and characteristics. "Nations" are not natural or fixed. Once the nation became a significant conceptual mode of organizing people, how and by what means the national quest for self-determination expressed itself and the degree of congruence with the state varied considerably. Early manifestations in popular anti-colonial movements were followed by newly independent state leaders keen on defining and crafting nations within their boundaries. They did so through a range of tools along a spectrum of "civic" types of political values at one end to defining an "ethnic" core at another. Markers of difference varied from language or religion to identification of core ethnic characteristics. They elevated and defined "national characteristics" and weaved them into a whole host of policies designed to further solidify the nations they defined. In the process of doing so, they expanded the reach of the state, both through territorial presence and governance tools, thereby increasing central state power in part to weaken resistance to its nation-building efforts. In doing so, they fostered responses from groups which, for a variety of historical reasons, defined alternative "peripheral" or "minority" nationalism in resistance to the state's homogenizing policies. Such a premise guides this analysis of nationalism in Southeast Asia. The argument points to a link between the initial attempt by state leaders to construct nations in the post-independence period and later sub-state nationalist movements. Southeast Asia offers further refinement to the variety and forms of nationalisms that arose, as the subsequent sections discuss.

State Nationalism and Sub-state Nationalist Mobilization

In its earliest forms, nationalism in Southeast Asia first inspired anti-colonial movements before it became a primary tool of newly independent states to build unity and loyalty within their boundaries. State leaders defined the nation, whether out of a reconstructed history of struggle against imperial rule or as cultural heritage of some distant historical past, with the primary objective of reducing ethnic, religious, or cultural differences within state boundaries and enhancing a constructed vision of a new nation for whom their states were being crafted.

Yet, newly independent regimes in Southeast Asia converged toward state nationalism in ways that produced limited inclusion. Nationalism took a variety of forms toward the end of colonial rule. Once independent, the new leaders converged in adopting state nationalism to consolidate their regime, secure the gains achieved in past post-colonial struggles, build new and prosperous states for newly emancipated "nations," or continue guarding against remnants of colonial rule. These agendas were built on strong nationalist feelings in some cases but were much more state-directed in others.

While many Southeast Asian state leaders espoused nationalism, and adopted trajectories quite similar to newly minted leaders elsewhere, they did so in a region where ethnic, religious, and cultural differences were deep (Liow, 2016, Reid, 2010). It can be particularly difficult to generalize about national-ism's impact and expression across Southeast Asia, given the variation in terms of pre-colonial notions of power and its relationship to territory, vastly different forms of statehood and scale of political units, as well as very heterogenous experiences of colonialism (Lieberman, 2003, Reid, 2010). Furthermore, sev-eral European powers occupied different sub-regions of Southeast Asia, some layered over other powers preceding them, and Siam standing alone as avoiding colonial rule. Anti-colonial nationalist movements varied as well in their polit-ical activities from revolutionary war to gradualist negotiation.

At the risk of overgeneralizing or simplifying, the region nevertheless saw the rise of state nationalisms that converged around the view that the state repre-sented a unique nation. States used a number of tools to define cultural markers of their nations and deepen their socialization among diverse populations. The homogenizing tendencies varied in their approach, or their substance.

As I show in the cases of Indonesia, the Philippines, Thailand and Burma/Myanmar, without exaggerating any predictive outcomes, state nationalism reached limits and ultimately contributed to creating or fueling sub-state nation-alisms, mostly through two pathways. First, the more inclusive and bottom-up forms eventually fared better in accommodating sub-state nationalism but often with decades of conflict after states deepened their definitions and cultural markers of the nation, which made some groups feel excluded. These processes were layered over anti-colonial nationalism that varied from claiming high degree of inclusion to deepening identity differences on the one hand, while also varying from mostly bottom-up movements to primarily driven by a small group of nationalist leaders and, in the case of Thailand, by the state. Second, when states used authoritarian and repressive policies, they ultimately fueled sub-state nationalism rather than eliminated it. State leaders tended to use particularly strong repressive tools, especially under authoritarian regimes, against groups that resisted being included in their definition of the nation, mostly fueling rather than reducing sub-state nationalist responses (Bertrand, 2021:12–13).

Anti-colonial Nationalism and Revolutionary Movements

Nationalist movements upon which independent states crafted their new nations are rooted in anti-colonial struggles. They emerged, evolved, and crystallized through a mix of shared experience, collective action, and leadership. Colonialism increasingly tied together peoples with little in common and, through shared experience of discrimination and oppression developed a sense of belonging together as a community.

But agency and conscious crafting of a nationalist project played significant roles even in those movements that seemed to emerge from a new consciousness from below. Revolutionary struggles, as the most vivid form of collective action, helped to create mass followings, identify a focal objective of freeing oneself from colonial rule, and enhancing the brotherhood and collective spirit that would become a nationalist one.

Finally, nationalist leaders themselves organized, framed and gave institutional expression to their goals of crafting nations. They also struggled against competing narratives by which "other" substantive definitions of the nation, and criteria of membership, would arise. There was therefore no teleological necessity to the emergence and form of nationalism in Southeast Asia, nor were the boundaries and criteria of nations either obvious or inevitable.

This section discusses how Southeast Asian cases, coming from quite varied colonial situations, converged toward forming nationalist movements to solidify the struggle against colonial rule, consolidate unity in the case of Siam, or to forge a common identity in anticipation of independence. The extent to which these struggles resulted in highly inclusive movements laid the basis for future state nationalism. Indonesia and the Philippines were the most inclusive, and their revolutionary component mobilized support at the grassroots. By contrast, Siam's monarchy adopted a new nationalist agenda in its quest to consolidate unity, and transform its basis of legitimacy, while the Burmese nationalist movement failed to be sufficiently inclusive of ethnic minority groups.

The "nation" as a modular form had its origins in the Americas and Europe, but still emerged in some cases from growing awareness of shared experience by groups of equal members, with a common purpose of freeing oneself from oppressive rule. As Anderson noted, this "last wave" saw the emergence of new identities as "Indonesian" or "Filipino," forming the basis of an identity as "nation." This consciousness developed mostly among native colonial administrators who realized the limits of their progression within colonial ranks and came increasingly to see their shared destiny despite disparate origins; it was enhanced by emerging literati, columnists, and novelists who used a shared language to increasingly express their common plight and aspirations (Anderson, 1991).

The proto-typical case was Indonesia, which had no clear sense of shared identity prior to Dutch colonial rule. The vast archipelago had once seen larger states, such as the little-known kingdoms of Majapahit or Mataram, but these periods of relatively larger amalgamated territories and shared rule were short-lived, while most of the precolonial period saw instead more localized and shifting kingdoms ruling over a vast array of peoples speaking different languages and often fighting one another. The territorial boundaries of the Dutch colony, which occupied more or less extensively the archipelago from the sixteenth to twentieth century, defined an idea of shared space upon which a small, mostly Dutch educated elite of colonial bureaucrats built the idea of "Indonesia." This idea spread through pamphlets, novels, and other forms of written works in Malay, which was a regional lingua franca that became elevated as the shared language from which a common consciousness would arise. The declaration of the Indonesian Youth Pledge in 1928 of Bahasa Indonesia as the language of the emerging nation was a key moment in Indonesia's nationalist movement and provided a basis for shared identity that rejected an association with a particular group, and created the ability to mobilize around an imagined community of the various peoples under the Dutch colonial administration (Reid, 2010:109). The nationalist movement and the idea of the Indonesian nation then progressed through the active spread by nationalist leaders such as the eventual first president, Soekarno, and others such as Mohammad Hatta, who formed the Indonesian National Party (PNI) as an expression of this emerging nation (Anderson, 1991, Kahin and Anderson, 2018:37–40; 90–100).

But there were some tensions in the mobilizational basis of this community, and the shared understanding of a common nation. Most significantly, alternative attempts to build a community around Islamic identity competed directly with the more inclusive appeals, based on Bahasa Indonesia, that Soekarno and his compatriots in the PNI propagated (Formichi, 2010; Kahin and Anderson,

2018). The rise and evolution of a nationalist imaginary around the idea of "Indonesia" therefore was not only made possible by the technological, literary, and linguistic transmission that built common awareness, but also through the active crafting of the community and its scope by leaders such as Soekarno, in contested terrain against those espousing community through the Islamic *ummah*.

Revolution also contributed significantly to binding colonial subjects and crystallizing a common goal of establishing a new political structure for a liberated political community as "Indonesian." In earlier work, Anderson had emphasized the crucial role played by youth groups that wholeheartedly espoused the common nationalist trope but also the revolutionary momentum that began as Japanese occupiers left the archipelago (Anderson, 1972). As Anthony Reid noted, "[t]he blood of revolutionary martyrs helped to sacralise the flag, the independence declaration and the sacred sites of the dead" (Reid, 2010:26). Its impact made possible a unitary Indonesia under a strong sense of nationhood that state rituals and museums would reinforce over time (Reid, 2010:212).

Filipino nationalism also arose in part from the common experience under Spanish colonial rule. Revolutionary action helped the mobilization and spread of this new awareness, but its failure and lack of sustained leadership produced a less cohesive and goal-oriented expression of a nationalist project. The idea of a "Filipino" nation nevertheless emerged and would become the basic community associated with the independent state.

Educated elites, many of whom were novelists and newspaper editors, formed the "Propaganda Movement" that was able to articulate a common community of "Filipinos." They rose above previously distinct categories of *indios* (natives), *mestizos,* Chinese, Igorots, and Moros (Sidel, 2021:22, Vu, 2013:261). The movement and its ideas then spread to a broader educated elite, commonly known as *ilustrados*.

A revolutionary movement contributed to the nationalist narrative but failed in its quest to dislodge colonial rule. As John Sidel indicates, while the common narrative blends this revolutionary impetus with nationalist *ilustrados*, they are analytically distinct. What became known as the Katipunan has its roots in a "long tradition of millenarian rebellions . . . .and indigenous understandings of charismatic authority and a moral economy rooted in guarantees of subsistence" (Sidel, 2021:23). The peasants, artisans, fishermen, and sugarcane workers that formed the movement's core were "largely illiterate, unschooled and unversed in Spanish," and would never have read the newspapers and materials circulated by the *ilustrado* elite (Sidel, 2021:23). The Katipunan failed against colonial rule in the late nineteenth century but Filipino nationalism would nevertheless draw on both this revolutionary imaginary and the discourse from the *ilustrado* elite.

Burmese nationalism diverged significantly from the experiences of Indonesia and the Philippines as British colonialism more strongly divided the Bamar Buddhist majority group from the highland minority groups. Colonial policies contributed to reifying ethnicity and religion, upon which nationalism built. After abolishing the Burmese monarchy, the British recruited mostly minority groups within the colonial administrative and military structures, while ignoring previous Burmese institutions and agencies. In addition, they administered Burma as a province of India, while splitting Burma proper from the minority Frontier Areas (Taylor, 2005:269–276).

Religion also contributed to deepening the ethnic divide. Christian missionaries had accompanied the spread of colonial rule. Religious conversion mainly occurred among ethnic minority groups, thereby layering religious over ethnic divides. While Buddhist monks had been strongly involved in education, they were further displaced not only by the so-called secular colonial educational system but also in areas where Christian religious orders expanded their broader educational role (Taylor, 2005:269–276).

It is not surprising that, as a result of these policies as Taylor contends, nationalist aspirations blended with ethnic and religious identities in ways that prevented a single, anti-colonial nationalism from emerging. Nationalist organizations such as the Young Men's Buddhist Association reacted against colonial policies that they perceived to be direct attacks on Buddhism and Burmese culture (Taylor, 2005:269–276).

Finally, nationalism in Thailand was primarily state-driven from the outset. Its trajectory was not dissimilar to what Anderson observed as "official nationalism" in early European forms, when monarchies under threat from rising discontent appropriated the nationalist modular form, espoused local vernaculars, and sought legitimacy based on the "nation," rather than divine right to rule. In Thailand, the monarchy similarly used nationalism to reinvent the bases of its legitimacy.

Thongchai Winichakul wrote of Thai nationhood emerging out of a history of state-building. The history of state-making and imagining an identity as "Thai" were deeply intertwined, and involved mapping out territory alongside redefining the community. King Chulalongkorn was increasingly concerned with maintaining control over his rule as French and British colonial empires expanded throughout continental Southeast Asia. Prior to the late nineteenth century, Siamese kings ruled through networks of control over people, with only vague regard for territory. It was the pressure from European expansion, as well as the mapping technologies they brought, that increasingly transformed the

Siamese concept of state into one associated with boundaries and territorial control. Building and mapping these borders came to delimit the community of "Thai" that the monarchy increasingly defined. Using monarchy and Buddhism as core elements of "nation," the state proceeded to use Thai language and cultural symbols to create a "Thai" nation, and to strengthen the "other" relative to the Thai "we-ness" (Winichakul, 1994). As Thongchai sums up: "The first form of nationalism in early 20th century Siam was what I call royal nationalism, a nationalism defined by loyalty to the monarchy" (Winichakul, 2008:584).

As these four cases illustrate, while nationalism captured the imagination of anti-colonial rebellious movements as well as monarchical leaders seeking new forms of legitimacy, its expression and mode of transmission in Southeast Asia was quite varied. Revolution and bottom-up mobilization inspired nationalist narratives to bind together the resistance to colonial rulers in Indonesia and the Philippines. While one succeeded, the other faltered, but the basic characteristics of an "Indonesian" or "Filipino" nation remained. Nationalism inspired similar anti-colonial, independence movements among young Buddhist Bamar in Burma, with only late attempts to articulate some common anti-colonial objectives with ethnic minorities, and little common struggle that would craft a broader, more inclusive concept of the Burmese nation. Finally, Siam followed the pre-emptive "official nationalisms" that Anderson had observed among some of the decaying European monarchies. With colonial pressures forcing reform, the Thai monarchy laid the basis of the Thai nation and its characteristics. In spite of these different origins and expressions, these nationalisms were available for post-colonial state leaders to use, modify, and shape to strengthen their own conceptions of nation, whether to nurture stronger bonds of loyalty and legitimacy or strengthen unity. But they started with very different degrees of inclusiveness and modes of nationalist mobilization, which had consequences for how state nationalism was later received among diverse groups in post-independence states.

State Nationalism and Sub-state Nationalist Responses

When states gained independence, new leaders faced a number of challenges to build representative institutions, bureaucracies and security forces, but many were also concerned about creating a unified community that would support and recognize the legitimacy of the new states. Nationalism remained a powerful source upon which new leaders could draw to seek legitimacy, address what they might perceive as weak sense of loyalty to the new state, or a tool to bolster support for their regime. The transfer of nationalist mobilization against colonial rulers to one in support of new states was not automatic, linear, nor necessarily as strong. Some state leaders chose to tap into the powerful imagery and discourse that brought them to power. Others tried to craft a more unified nation, or adopted nationalist policies to counter emerging challenges. The emancipatory role that nationalism and its corollary liberation movements played in some cases became tools for state leaders to unify their peoples, gain legitimacy, and consolidate new regimes' power.

As leaders expanded the use of state nationalism, they built on the foundations that were left from anti-colonial nationalist movements. The latter also set some limits to the mobilizational effectiveness of discourses and policies that state nationalists deployed. In cases such as Indonesia and the Philippines, appeals to anti-colonial struggles and shared suffering under colonial rule continued to resonate with large masses that had participated in emancipation movements. But these appeals were supplemented with cultural, linguistic, or other policies designed to define more deeply and entrench their conceptions of nation, once the common focal point of removing colonial authorities was gone. State leaders inheriting an already state-led nationalism, such as in the case of Siam, or where anti-colonial movements failed to include large portions of groups within the new state boundaries, often adopted strong policies designed to define and deepen loyalty to the nation. They faced uncertainty regarding the degree of adherence to the nation and often feared that a lack of common shared identity might lead to fractious politics.

In this section, I show that as state nationalism expanded, it created or exacerbated the exclusion of certain groups. In reaction, some groups that were marginalized developed new sub-state nationalist identities and political agendas. In a few cases, where sub-state nationalist mobilization had already developed, state nationalist policies contributed to consolidating and intensifying it.

In cases below, I discuss two factors that create state nationalism's marginalization impact: First, the more the state defined and enforced certain cultural and ethnic markers for its conception of nation, the more it encountered groups that resisted being included. Second, authoritarian tools, such as assimilation and repression, contributed to intensifying sub-state nationalist formation and intensity. These two factors combined were present in all cases of sub-state nationalism that are discussed below.

There are a few additional factors, however, that are also crucial. First, only groups that were territorially concentrated could respond with sub-state nationalist movements. While other groups might have also been excluded or marginalized, if they were not sufficiently concentrated in a territory, it would be difficult to construct a sub-state nationalist movement. Second, the perception of marginalization is key, not only objective criteria of cultural differentiation.

For groups that did not participate in anti-colonial nationalist mobilization, the perception of exclusion from the nation could be even stronger. For instance, Papuans never participated in the nationalist movement against the Dutch, but the Acehnese did. State nationalist policies were seen as even more marginalizing than Acehnese who had originally adhered to the idea of an Indonesian nation. Finally, no sub-state nationalism just emerged, it required leaders who crafted organizations and articulated new identities in response to perceived grievances. But leadership in itself is not sufficient; nationalist appeals resonate when groups feel marginalized by state policies and particularly when repressed.

I then turn to understand why, in two cases, sub-state nationalist movements were greatly reduced. I show that two factors were key, but both needed to be present: i) some degree of explicit recognition of the distinctiveness of groups; ii) the institutional flexibility toward regional/local territorial units. But accommodating only one dimension, although leading to periods of less tension, never produced lasting results.

The starting point for all four cases was already different. Indonesia had the highest claims to inclusion, given a bottom-up revolutionary movement that was built upon an ideal of "Indonesia" as a new nation composed of many different ethnic groups. While "Filipino" had a similarly inclusive dimension in the earlier failed revolutionary movement, neither later revolution nor anti-colonial movement managed to continue developing a broader nation that could fully include Moro Muslims. The end of colonial rule left Burma with a deep tension between creating an overarching "Burmese" nation and recognizing ethnic differences. Neither the Panglong agreement, nor the first constitution, resolved these tensions, by which the anti-colonial nationalist movement was primarily a majority Bamar quest for freedom from colonial rule, while ethnic groups from the Highlands joined the Bamar under a promise of recognition of their distinctive ethnicity and territory. Thai nationalism claimed inclusiveness but had already been state-directed since King Chulalongkorn's reign, and regimes following the 1932 coup continued to impose the "Thai" nation as an all-inclusive concept.

At the time of independence, or in the case of Thailand after the Second World War when colonial threats were waning, the more inclusive Indonesia should have managed best internal differences, while "Filipino" and "Thai" certainly had potential. In the Philippines, state nationalists would need to nurture the inclusion of Moros, who had collaborated with the state while affirming their Muslim distinction. In Thailand, with no bottom up movement for a Thai nation, it would remain uncertain the degree to which imposing Thai as a common culture was well received. Burmese leaders had the most difficult choice of seeking more cohesion through accommodating difference or adopting a stronger state nationalist approach to foster unity. Yet, Burmese had the most unique possibility to follow a different pathway that, at the outset, might have followed through with cultural recognition and territorial accommodation.

In all of these cases, whether because of the insecurity of gaining new states or perceived need to foster unique and strong nations to coincide with their states, state leaders adopted nationalist policies, coupled with repression when obstacles arose. The most significant pathway was cultural policy. Nationalist leaders often added layers of cultural markers and historical narratives to further strengthen the nation, oftentimes leading to exclusion and marginalization of particular groups. As Liow has argued, "religious nationalism" was particularly significant in the region, as religion offered an easily accessible, emotionally strong form of identity to seek loyalty. Such differentiation along religious lines in the case of the Philippines and Thailand, as he suggests, contributed to a reactive, sub-state nationalism that further entrenched religiously based differences in the cases of Bangsamoro and Malay Muslims (Liow, 2016). Religious identities also contributed to deepening sub-state nationalist movements in Burma, when state nationalist policies favored Buddhism.

In the Indonesian case, an overemphasis on Pancasila over Islam, and attempts to homogenize certain values and characteristics of being Indonesian, while socializing these through education and government programming, backfired most clearly in Aceh and Papua, where alternative sub-state nationalisms arose for different reasons. Repression of both groups intensified their resistance.

With gradual decolonization leaders in the Philippines used much less direct nationalist discourse but continued policies that strengthened the identification of "Filipino" national identity with the Christian majority. When Moros began to resist, increasing repression further solidified Moro nationhood in response.

Thai leaders tapped into the continuity of the monarchy against the backdrop of frequent military coups and leadership changes to uphold the primacy of King, Buddhism and Nation, and strengthen the project of "Thainess" through education and linguistic assimilation. These policies led to strong resistance among Malay Muslims, and then an intensification of the Thai state's repressive policies.

Burmese leaders adopted increasingly homogenizing and assimilationist policies that reaffirmed the primacy of Buddhism, Burmese language, and the dominance of the Bamar. Early resistance from ethnic minority groups led to repression in response. When Ne Win seized the state and imposed a new regime, assimilation and repression intensified dramatically. Civil war set in for the following decades.

As the following sections will show in more detail, at various stages after the development of sub-state nationalisms, state leaders loosened some of their most restrictive policies along two pathways: more cultural recognition or some territorial accommodation. Yet, they mostly failed to reduce sub-state nationalist demands, as they were minimal concessions along one dimension, for the most part, and a far cry from giving actual recognition to sub-state nationalist groups, or responding adequately to their grievances. Where state nationalist policies contributed to intensifying or even prompting the rise of these sub-state nationalist movements, the reversal of these policies and lesser repression did not easily reduce resistance. Only the cases of Aceh and more recently the Moros have reduced violent outcomes and mobilization for independence. These were possible in part because of the bottom-up inclusion that supported original expressions of state nationalism, but most importantly because of significant departures from the past by recognizing and accommodating nationalist demands of these groups, while giving meaningful governance over territory they claimed to represent.

Indonesia

State nationalism has shaped and reinforced a vision of the Indonesian nation that reproduced Soekarno's original conception, while adding cultural layers to fend off challenges to its views. The state ideology of Pancasila became a convenient tool, alongside revolutionary imagery, for leaders to claim one single Indonesian nation, strengthen state symbols and discourses of the nation, as well as legitimize repressive approaches to counter opposition to the regime. Authoritarian rule under Guided Democracy in the late 1950s and early 1960s, as well as under Suharto's New Order regime (1965–1998), tapped into state nationalist discourse not only to deepen loyalty to the Indonesian nation but increasingly to induce compliance, inculcate particular notions of citizen obligation and loyalty to the regime, while providing a symbiotic association between repressive tools and nationalist rhetoric to placate opposition to the state or the regime.

Indonesia's state nationalism sought inclusiveness through Pancasila and recognizing ethnic diversity, but created tensions with those committed to the primacy of Islam as a basis of the nation and fueled the rise of sub-state nationalism in Aceh and Papua. In the first case, the ambiguity over cultural and territorial recognition, as well as tensions with Islamists, contributed to the alienation of parts of Aceh's elite, which then shaped an alternative sub-state nationalist narrative around its Islamic and unique cultural heritage. State repression sealed sub-state nationalism with the leadership of the Free Aceh

Movement steering decidedly toward nationalist goals while downplaying the Islamic dimension. In Papua, state nationalism became associated with forced inclusion to the Indonesian state, while repression and assimilation fueled a consolidation of sub-state Papuan nationalism and resistance.

Soekarno mastered the use of nationalist discourse, combined with revolutionary rhetoric, to solidify the concept of an Indonesian nation, particularly as a result of challenges to the state. In the early years of Indonesia's independence, Soekarno and the new Republic challenged Dutch attempts to create a federal state along ethnic lines. The unitary movement rejected more decentralized governance and reaffirmed the primacy of the single Indonesian nation over any recognition of ethnic differences. When the Republic of South Maluku attempted to secede, the Indonesian armed forces successfully repressed the rebellion. The subsequently strong Moluccan elite's affirmation of loyalty to the Republic sealed the initial conception of the unitary state representing a single, Indonesian nation. Subsequent regionalist rebellions over the following decade were again crushed militarily, with the accompanying justification of preserving unity and the nation (Kahin, 1985, Kahin and Anderson, 2018).

There was strong support both at the elite and mass level, however, for Soekarno's nationalist vision as well as the military's defense of the unitary state. State nationalist discourse tapped into decades of mobilization that reflected the common sense of shared experience and community giving rise to anti-colonial nationalism from the 1920s onwards. Sustained mobilization and layering of state nationalist "victories" against state opponents reinforced the bottom-up ties that Anderson observed as the basis of the imagined Indonesian nation. As Leifer noted, nationalism developed both as a "negative" reaction to racial distinctions of the colonial border but also as a "positive" reaction to the territorial boundaries that the Dutch had created. Together, these formed the basis of the more "civic" inclination of Indonesian nationalism that resisted any reference to an "ethnic" core, as it would necessarily clash with the reality of Indonesia's diversity. Soekarno nurtured the idea of a struggle to inscribe nationalism within a longer range and sustained anti-colonial and anti-imperialist goal. In what Leifer suggests was a "romantic" phase of nationalism, Soekarno claimed an "archipelagic principle" to justify the continued fight against the Dutch in West New Guinea and the British in Malaya, both external struggles mostly aimed at consolidating domestic unity of the nation (Leifer, 2000:158–166).

Despite strong ties that nationalist imagery and revolutionary rhetoric fostered, Soekarno's vision of nationalism was challenged by Islamist discourse. As an alternative source of unity for the Indonesian community, in many respects appeals to the shared Islamic faith also aimed at building an

"Indonesian" rather than a broader Muslim community. While not wholly anathema to a nationalist frame, therefore, it nevertheless represented a different base of community ties, with religious dimensions competing with more secular, cultural or linguistic ties that Soekarno's nationalism sought to foster.

The rise of Islamist challenges to Soekarno's nationalist vision was most significant in the Darul Islam movement. It formed ties between groups in South Sulawesi, West Java and Aceh, that challenged the Indonesian state and its original constitution. It certainly had existing roots among some nationalists who had viewed Islam as stronger than shared colonial experience or shared language to build common ties. Political parties that had formed around the banner of Islam, such as Masjumi, had made strong appeals at the time of the revolution against the returning Dutch to constitutionalize an Islamic state. When the 1945 constitution was adopted, some Islamist groups and parties felt betrayed by the last-minute withdrawal from the preamble of seven words obligating Muslims to follow shariah law. Darul Islam was a violent rebellion that sought to overthrow the Indonesian state based on Pancasila, the state ideology enshrined in the constitution, and replace it with an Islamic state. Masjumi and some other Islamist parties meanwhile challenged the quasi-secularist Pancasila state through formal institutional structures, by running in elections with an Islamist platform and promoting an Islamist alternative in the Constituent Assembly, where proponents of alternative visions of nationalism and Islam disagreed on the basis of the Indonesian state (Dijk, 1981).

Soekarno and his nationalist allies had been concerned that enshrining Islamic law would threaten a more inclusive conception of the nation. With Eastern Indonesia having majority Christian areas, they feared that some regions would reject the new nation. The "Jakarta Charter," whose draft of the constitution's preamble had included formal obligation for Muslims to follow shariah law, was modified immediately prior to the adoption of the 1945 Constitution. Instead, the preamble retained Pancasila and adopted as its first principle Belief in One and Only God, which allowed to enshrine religion as an important value while not specifying any particular one (Boland, 1971:27–35).

For Masjumi, and the Darul Islam rebellion, such a compromise denied the fact that Muslims were an overwhelming majority. The Constituent Assembly, formed in 1955 to discuss a new constitution, never produced results as parties remained deeply divided on the relative role of Islam, nationalism, and Pancasila as the basis of the state. These divisions occurred against the backdrop of the Darul Islam rebellion that managed to continue its fight for more than a decade after independence (Feith, 1962:212–214). While in the end, the armed forces defeated it, the rebellion nevertheless represented a significant challenge to a particular conception of the nation that would remain alive for the following decades.

The implications of the Islamist challenge were two-fold. For the most part, it would defy a more secularist, non-Islamic state while maintaining a unifying view of the Indonesian nation. Islamists espoused Islamic law for Muslims, and an Islamic state for the Indonesian nation. This stream of nationalism remained an important trope in the evolving discourse on the Indonesian state and nation. The second implication was more complex. The Darul Islam in particular, and to some extent Masjumi, was based in particular regions and among specific ethnic groups. Some of the rebellion had a strongly defensive, regionalist base that resented the dominant nationalist vision that was supported mostly by Javanese. While it would be an exaggeration to suggest that either movement or party were secessionist or even strongly ethnically based, they certainly maintained aspects of unity among specific Muslim majority groups against the dominant view of the place of religion (Formichi, 2012). Acehnese, West Javanese, Makassarese viewed their societies as "more Islamic" than those of other ethnic groups. They tapped into such ethnic, regional distinctions to justify their mobilization against what was sometimes seen as a "Javanese" dominated state. A regionalist rebellion in 1957 declared an alternative Revolutionary Government of the Republic of Indonesia, also based mostly in Sumatra and Sulawesi. Although it aimed at forming an alternative government for all of Indonesia and was not secessionist, it was nevertheless protesting the over-centralization of the central government, and its tendencies to reinforce the centre and unity over the varied needs of regions (Harvey, 1977). By the late 1950s, there was therefore potential for some ethnic groups to challenge the strong centralized state, based on Soekarno's views of a strong, unified Indonesian nation. Islam, regionalism, and ethnicity were all potential bases of these challenges.

Tensions in the substantive criteria for the nation notwithstanding, there was consensus about its broad inclusiveness. Islamists questioned its basis but adhered to the notion of an inclusive Indonesian nation, even if they remained ambiguous about the implications for non-Muslim groups. Furthermore, most regions that had contested state centralization did not develop sub-state nationalist responses. Most ethnic groups adhered and wholly identified with the Indonesian nation, in part because leaders' substantive use of state nationalism did not deny their ability to use their language or advance their culture, within the bounds of defined non-ethnicized territorial units and overarching primacy of the Indonesian language. The bottom up, revolutionary unity from the past supported enthusiastic acceptance of the Indonesian nation. ·

State nationalism, based on Pancasila, became enshrined in the Constitution and in policies designed to strengthen the nation. Pancasila was mostly a set of values, but the first principle of "Belief in One God" maintained a religious dimension without giving primacy to Islam. Under the New Order regime, however, school curricula and civil service training courses expanded values and norms derived from Pancasila, including certain behaviours and cultural characteristics of being "Indonesian." It reified certain heroes of Indonesian history, and reinvented others as part of a longer claim to a mythical past stretching back to empires of Majapahit and Mataram. Ethnic differences were recognized but given secondary place, denied any territorial or adminis-trative representation, and merely allowed certain cultural and linguistic accom-modations. Local cultures were even reinvented to fit the mold of New Order policy and how it designed its views of cultural diversity within the unity of the Indonesian nation (Pemberton, 1994). For the most part, ethnic groups across Indonesia accepted this hierarchy and clearly espoused the vision and primacy of the Indonesian nation, even if some might have resented certain aspects of how it was propagated in state policies. The inclusiveness of Indonesian nationalism, and degree of acculturation that was imposed did not threaten the perceived core identities of most ethnic groups. And since few resisted, they were not subjected to repression in the way that Acehnese or Papuans were.

Alternative, sub-state nationalist movements arose in Aceh and Papua, mostly because state nationalism failed to accommodate distinctive features of these groups and used repressive or assimilationist policies when conflict appeared. The first, in Aceh, had its origins in the Darul Islam rebellion. Acehnese joined the rebellion in support of an Islamic state but also regionalist grievances underlie the mobilization. The new Republic had denied Aceh its own province originally, likely because of state insecurity as Acehnese had a very strong sense of historical distinctiveness. The nationalist turn would come later, once Acehnese had been given a province, but territorial accommo-dation remained largely meaningless. With added repression during the New Order regime of President Suharto, the leadership of the Free Aceh Movement gained strong support for its sub-state nationalist alternative.

The second was a strong reaction to Soekarno's external expression of nationalism, designed to unify the archipelago as one Indonesian nation. His claim to West New Guinea continued the struggle against the Dutch, but over a former colony that in fact had few ties to the previous Dutch East Indies. Having not participated in the revolution, or adhered to the nationalist move-ment during the anti-colonial struggle, Papuans did not have any sense of commonality with other groups in Indonesia. Papuan nationalists developed their own quest for a shared nation from the large number of tribal groups in

West New Guinea, and viewed subsequent attempts by Indonesia to quell their alternative nationalism and include them in the Indonesian nation as neo-colonial. When the New Order regime added repression and assimilationist policies, Papuans' alternative sub-state nationalism grew stronger (Bertrand, 2004, Drooglever, 2009).

Aceh is in many ways the litmus test of Indonesian nationalism. With a unique history at the tip of the archipelago, Aceh was a stop-over for maritime trading. As a result, generations of settlers made it exceptionally mixed and diverse. Yet, it would emerge as having one of the strongest claims to unique identity against the rise of a strongly centralizing Indonesian nationalism. Acehnese nationalism crystallized its identity, and provided a strong source of mobilizational capital.

Two original paths taken by Indonesian nationalists laid the basis for revolt. The first was an attempt by the first government of Indonesia to prevent a potential rise of regional identity in Aceh. After all, it was one of the regions that had put up an effective rebellion against the Dutch, thereby avoiding the much longer colonization in Java or the Moluccas. The temporary 1950 consti-tution created ten provinces, with Aceh being included into North Sumatra instead of obtaining its own status as a province. Some of the Acehnese elite resented this lack of recognition, particularly since they considered the partici-pation of Aceh in the anti-Dutch revolution as having been key in securing Indonesia's independence and creating the new Republic. Acehnese ironically refused Dutch offers of a federal state and rallied around the unitary state and the Republic. Yet, once denied a province, regionalist sentiments surfaced (Morris, 1984:180–181).

The second path was Soekarno's compromise to religious minorities in denying Islamists a new constitution based on Islamic law for Muslims. The adoption of Pancasila was not well received in Aceh, where a new elite of *ulama* replaced the long dominant *uleebalang*, aristocratic elite that had remained strong throughout colonial rule. The *ulama* gained influence and local power partly by reframing Acehnese as a strongly Muslim society, and using Islam as a source of political mobilization and support. Acehnese *ulama* therefore considered the modification to the Jakarta Charter as a broken promise of an Islamic state (Reid, 1979:8–11).

Partly fueled by the combination of these factors, Acehnese leader Daud Beureueh and other Acehnese ulama joined the Darul Islam in 1953. They shared a continued commitment to the Republic but with the objective of establishing an Islamic state. Yet, they maintained a regionalist identity that would subsequently shed much of the Islamist objective and develop instead into a nationalist movement.

Islamic values played a key role in the mobilizational strength of the Darul Islam movement. At the elite level, Daud Beureueh and other ulama certainly led much of the rebellion but they were joined by civil servants and high military officers who shared the general resentment toward Jakarta's centralizing tendencies. As Sjamsuddin has argued, thousands of villagers also joined and helped to support the rebellion, mostly inspired by the ulama's leadership and the Islamic values they were attempting to uphold. From their perspective, there were really no grievances based on socioeconomic losses, so it was the vision of Aceh's identity that seemed prevalent at the time (Sjamsuddin, 1985:177).

Yet, the failure of Darul Islam closed the door to an Islamic state, at least in the short term, and shifted Acehnese away from Indonesia-wide goals. The elite, as well as many Acehnese, began to internalize the military's response as repressive and unappreciative of Acehnese as fully committed Indonesians. The failed rebellion also served to highlight even more the regionalist grievances that underlie some of the mobilization. And finally, the elite itself became less consolidated as those former civil servants and military officers that had initially supported the ulama's vision now turned to an alternative view of Aceh. Some of them would come to accept the Indonesian compromise and work within its parameters (Bertrand, 2004:167–169).

The shift from some regionalist grievances to an Acehnese nationalist movement was a direct result of the Indonesian state's policies to uphold its vision of the Indonesian nation. As Aspinall has convincingly argued, nationalist entrepreneurs, most significantly Hasan di Tiro, were able to craft and communicate "a collective action frame justifying revolt." While grievances were present, and they would grow in light of state policies, they were reinterpreted and communicated to Acehnese through this new aspiration of a free Aceh, in a continual process of persuasion (Aspinall, 2020:51). While Hasan Di Tiro's articulation of these new goals was critical, he was also able to tap into two distinct networks of support, namely young intellectuals and professionals with whom he shared a background, as well as some former supporters of the Darul Islam. He could cast Aceh as having had a long history of independent statehood, interrupted by Dutch and subsequently Javanese colonialism (Aspinall, 2020:69). The call to arms and formation of the Free Aceh Movement (Gerakan Aceh Merdeka, GAM) in 1976 institutionalized the move away from Islamist goals and gave birth to clear nationalist aspirations for an independent state (Aspinall, 2020:217).

The second and third waves of GAM's mobilization showed growing strength of Acehnese nationalism, in response to escalating repression. State policies reflecting limits to Indonesian nationalism's accommodation contributed significantly to the spread of support. Ironically, di Tiro's first attempt at mobilizing GAM in 1976 seemed to have little resonance within the broader Acehnese population. The second rebellion in 1989 showed great popular support but, more importantly, the state's response most significantly crystallized the movement. Grievances certainly contributed, as Acehnese experienced a growing sense that external forces were profiting from Aceh with little evidence of local gains. The armed forces guarded industrial facilities, and business groups in conjunction with the Indonesian state oil company Pertamina controlled lucrative, and visible, LNG plants while the vast majority of Acehnese remained poor. But the Indonesian armed forces' brutal repression of the rebellion, followed by a decade of military occupation, repression, and widespread operations to "root out" GAM fueled nationalist sentiment and consolidated GAM's widespread popularity (Kell, 1995).

While Suharto's authoritarian regime often used repression against opposition groups, its scale and widespread use in Aceh eroded any sense of belonging to a common Indonesian nation. In the 1990s, the Indonesian government declared Aceh a Military Operations Zone. Military campaigns, sweeping operations in villages to weed out GAM supporters, and strong policies designed to provide resources and integrate Aceh as a province equal to others created more renewed support for Acehnese nationalism than significant loyalty or compliance with the Indonesian state's vision of homogeneity. It is not surprising that GAM came to represent freedom from oppression, and its goals of an independent Aceh were widely supported.

Furthermore, the regime's attempts to minimally accommodate Acehnese were meaningless in relation to continued repression. While Aceh had gained status as a "special region" in 1959, during the highly centralized regime of President Suharto from 1965 to 1998 the designation was meaningless, with no real powers devolved to the region beyond the administrative deconcentration present in every other province, nor any particular distinct cultural, linguistic or religious accommodations.

When the Suharto regime collapsed, popular support for Acehnese nationalism became clear. Hundreds of thousands joined protests in November 1999 asking for a referendum on independence. When these demands fell on deaf ears, the resumption of war with GAM resumed but, this time, the latter enjoyed widespread support as it consolidated demands for independence and claimed its place as the primary representative of Acehnese aspirations. This third rebellion became the longest and the most deadly, despite the collapse of the previous authoritarian regime and the beginning of a democratic period in Indonesia. With the armed forces unable to defeat GAM, negotiations were held to craft a pathway toward peaceful resolution. At this point, the state's recognition of Acehnese nationalism could hardly be denied (Bertrand, 2004:173–182).

Suharto's successor Habibie attempted to appease Acehnese demands for a referendum on independence by offering Islamic law, alongside a few economic infrastructural projects. But this gesture failed to quell nationalist demands. After civil war resumed on a large-scale in 2000, it became clear that previous decades of successive attempts to crush GAM failed. Once again, the Indonesian state attempted to provide more territorial powers and some cultural recognition by providing Aceh in 2002 with the status of "special autonomy," but these measures again fell short of what had become GAM's much stronger claims, backed by very strong local support for its nationalist vision.

When GAM and the Indonesian state negotiated a peace agreement in 2005, which became the Law on Aceh in 2006, the notion of the unitary state expressing the unity of the Indonesian nation was modified. The Constitution did not recognize Aceh specifically as being different from other provinces but allowed for laws that would recognize and enshrine institutional differences reflecting the distinctiveness of particular regions. The Law on Aceh did so by providing some symbolic recognition of local titles, such as the designation of the governor with an Acehnese title, and used Acehnese language to refer to rules and regulations. More significantly, the law allowed Islamic law in divergence with other provinces. It also allowed local political parties, provided much more autonomy to the provincial government, and special fiscal allocations that were different from structures and resources in other provinces. In essence, the law created a form of asymmetry in the structures of Indonesian provinces that recognized the uniqueness of Aceh and resembled in substance, if not in its label, structures of asymmetric federalism. By doing so, without recognizing Aceh formally as a nation within Indonesia, it nevertheless recognized it in practice by providing high degrees of self-governance within structures of autonomy that resemble federal systems. This ambiguity diverges from the historical idea of the Indonesian nation, while allowing both allegiances to co-exist (Bertrand, 2021:93–96).

Since its implementation in 2006, the decline of violence and near normal resumption of governance in Aceh suggests that Acehnese nationalism can be expressed in provincial institutions, while at the same time Acehnese possibly regaining loyalty if not strong adherence to the idea of being members of the Indonesian nation. By some accidental path of modified statecraft, Indonesia's institutions have been able to accommodate, if ambiguously, multiple overlapping nationalisms.

Meanwhile, at the other end of the archipelago, another nationalist movement arose in opposition to the Indonesian nation. Once again, the framing of grievances into a nationalist discourse was key. In this case, ironically, Dutch colonial authorities contributed to laying the base of Papuan nationalism in their own quest to resist Indonesia's claims to West New Guinea. Once articulated in nationalist terms, Papuan grievances against the Indonesian state intensified, and Papuan intellectuals and elites continued to craft its elements, including demands for independence, after West New Guinea was integrated to Indonesia.

Soekarno's claim to West New Guinea was inscribed in his archipelagic principle, by which he also had articulated aspirations for inclusion of parts of Malaya, in his "Konfrontasi" against the British. His anti-colonial brand of nationalism and his vision of the Indonesian nation had gone beyond the boundaries of the Dutch East Indies, and would eventually provide the justification for his successor, Suharto, to claim East Timor, which had been colonized by the Portuguese. Soekarno considered the lack of inclusion of West New Guinea, which had remained out of Indonesia at the time of Dutch cession of the colony in 1949 to the United States of Indonesia, as an incomplete process of decolonization and essential to finalizing the unity of the Indonesian nation (Bone, 1962:32).

Papuan nationalists, however, responded to these claims with their own quest for independence on the basis of a nascent Papuan nation, and in resistance to new Indonesian colonial ambitions. After Indonesia gained its independence in 1949, Dutch colonial authorities increasingly nurtured a new Papuan elite and helped to create the basis for a common "Papuan" nation. As with the rest of New Guinea, the western part was also populated by a large number of diverse groups, mostly governed by customary local rulers, speaking different languages and with many of them having few contacts with more than their neighbors. Coastal areas had more interactions both with each other, the Dutch as well as other parts of the archipelago but had formed neither common bonds with the rest of the archipelago to participate in movements that gave rise to Indonesian nationalism, nor much common bonds among each other. They certainly had few contacts with peoples in the inaccessible Highlands. In the 1950s, the Dutch built up a new educated and administrative elite, and prepared it for an eventual independent, or self-governed state. Indonesia's confrontational stance and its attempt to seize West New Guinea through a military campaign met with the Dutch authorities' further resolve to support a Papuan nation and state (Bone, 1962, Chauvel et al., 2004).

Papuan nationalism became deeply linked to the historical grievance of West New Guinea's integration to Indonesia. Under international pressure, the Dutch relinquished control of the colony to Indonesia in 1963, with the provision that the Indonesian government would hold a UN-mandated consultation to allow Papuans to choose integration or independence. The referendum was held in 1969 and was largely seen as illegitimate. Instead of a broad referendum, the Indonesian government selected 100 delegates who cast their votes in favour of integration. With West New Guinea under Indonesian military control and with the military also controlling the Indonesian government, the process of consultation and integration was widely considered to have been manipulated and the delegates intimidated into agreeing to integration. Papuans were further aggrieved when the United Nations approved the process and allowed their territory to be fully integrated and recognized as part of Indonesia. This process, the 1969 "Act of Free Choice," became Papuan nationalists' main source of historical grievance that they used to resist the Indonesian nation and state but also as a rallying cry for Papuan unity (Drooglever, 2009). Their vision of an alternative Papuan nation built on this grievance at forced integration; they rejected Indonesia's claims and articulated an alternative Papuan nationalism based as well on the deep cultural, social, and historical divide separating the Austronesian Papuans from the culturally distinct peoples' of the rest of the archipelago, including all Indonesians. These two elements formed the base of an alternative Papuan nationalism for several decades.

As with the Acehnese, Papuan nationalism grew stronger with an evolving Indonesian state nationalism that became narrower and backed by repressive policies. The integration of West New Guinea coincided with the consolidation of Suharto's New Order military regime. While military-led and clearly more authoritarian, the regime nevertheless was clearly inscribed into the path set by Soekarno's vision of an Indonesian nation. The Indonesian armed forces had been the primary actor in the resistance against the Dutch, and their formation from anti-colonial revolutionary forces strengthened their perceived role as guardian of the Indonesian nation and its unity. Above and beyond the military's desire to maintain its claimed territorial integrity, it was strengthened by Indonesian nationalism that legitimized, in its view, policies to forcibly assimilate Papuans into the Indonesian nation.

Suharto's regime therefore went one step beyond previous state attempts to further nationalist goals. While Soekarno had relied mainly on the strength of rhetorical and inspirational appeals, Suharto used military and state tools to implement concrete measures to solidify the Indonesian nation. Some of the more important ones included the adoption of a single, national curriculum reinforcing its version of history to reify and glorify the Indonesian nation. It was accompanied by cultural policies that recognized cultural groups and their distinction, but then redefined their character and included them within a broader narrative of their inclusion within the Indonesian nation. Perhaps the most visible monument to this vision was Suharto's wife's project of creating Taman Mini Indonesia, a museum intended to show (and reinvent) the multiple cultures forming the Indonesian nation. Finally, its homogenizing and centralizing policies from state administrative structures to nation-wide civil servant uniforms and codes of conduct created a uniform, state culture that the regime linked to Pancasila, the state ideology developed by Soekarno as a further expression of Indonesian nationalism.

When integrating West New Guinea, all of these new structures and cultural forms were implemented in the now renamed Irian Jaya, in itself a name derived from Sanskrit and again symbolically representing, in the Indonesian state's eyes, the nation. The educational curriculum reinforced the glory of military campaigns, including the state's reinvented view of its successful campaign to reintegrate West Irian (its name for West New Guinea) to the Indonesian whole. Papuans were stripped of local customary governance structures, forced to learn and use only Indonesian as official language, and made to adopt practices and customs then fully implemented elsewhere in Indonesia, even if they were deemed alien to local inhabitants (Bertrand, 2004:149–153).

Papuan resistance took a clear nationalist direction as soon as the Act of Free Choice occurred. Nationalist leaders and the educated elite all denounced the forced integration to Indonesia. They had already adopted a Papuan flag in preparation for their independence. The "Morning Star" flag, as it is called, became the most prominent symbol of nationalist resistance to Indonesia. For the following decades, recurrent mobilization and demonstrations often used the flag as a symbol of defiance, in the absence of significant military or political capacity to counter the overwhelming force of the Indonesian military and state. The main armed resistance, organized under the umbrella Organisasi Papua Merdeka (OPM), Free Papua Movement, was clearly nationalist in its character and goals, but hardly capable of mobilizing the kinds of resources required to mount a strong armed movement (Osborne, 1985).

Yet, as in Aceh, the Indonesian military's strong repressive approach only strengthened Papuan nationalism and resistance. While in the rest of Indonesia, state policies to strengthen nationalist goals were either enthusiastically sup-ported or, at worse, reluctantly accepted, they certainly did not provoke strong negative feelings. For many Papuans, state policies already denied their culture and livelihoods, and therefore they strongly rejected most of them as Indonesian colonial practices. Yet, military operations to weed out OPM supporters, repress potential resistance and tackle demonstrations made divisions even deeper. Only in Aceh, and in East Timor, did such intensive military operations occur. Other regions never experienced such degree of repression. Consequently, the military approach did little to "win the hearts and minds" of Papuans and, instead, deepened the sense of alienation and perception of being colonized (McGibbon, 2004).

More than two decades of democratic rule in Indonesia changed little to Papuan nationalist aspirations. While the democratic space allowed a new civilian movement to emerge and express more openly a Papuan nationalist discourse, it was soon repressed by security forces. Instead, the Indonesian state has continued to implement its vision of how Papua can participate in the Indonesian state with "special autonomy." Papuans never really saw "special autonomy" as legitimate because they were unable to negotiate either the terms of the recognition as a Papuan nation, nor various aspects of the powers and elements of self-governance that the autonomy law bestows upon the territory that is now divided into several provinces. Military campaigns and repression by security forces recurred regularly, in response to continued expression of rejection of Indonesia, denunciation of the Act of Free Choice, and state policies deemed to deny Papuans their rightful expression of nationhood. The resentment continued to run deep, and the rejection of inclusion into the Indonesian nation was strong (Bertrand, 2021:110–140).

In spite of its broadly inclusive nature, Indonesian nationalism still produced areas of exclusion, which fueled sub-state nationalist responses. At its origins, the bottom-up, revolutionary anti-colonial character of Indonesian nationalism ensured its broad appeal in constructing a state free from past colonial rule. The strains and limits came from the transformation of a revolutionary, anti-colonial form to a state nationalist project. Having acquired independence and state tools to implement, expand, and further deepen the state nationalist project, Indonesian leaders contributed to narrowing its inclusiveness and further defining its character in exclusionary terms. In the complex case of Aceh, the exclusion came early in the form of rejecting an Islamist expression of nationalism that had been present in earlier revolutionary forms. But Acehnese nationalism developed largely as a secular alternative to Indonesian nationalism, and constructed in response to state regionalist policies that failed to give recognition to Aceh's particular history and sense of its own identity. With layers of further grievances based in economic and political centralization, the articulation of a nationalist alternative took root as Hasan di Tiro and GAM offered a nationalist interpretation and solution to Aceh's grievances in the form of claims to independence. In the case of Papua, the exclusion was experienced at the outset. By contrast with Acehnese, Papuans had never participated in earlier, bottom-up movements that joined the common nationalist aspirations of early Indonesian revolutionaries. Instead, they were subjected to forced integration and subsequent policies that had already consolidated an Indonesian state nationalist project that had little space to accommodate Papuan differences, whether cultural, historical, or practical. Military backed state policies and repression further alienated and deepened both Acehnese and Papuan nationalisms.

It was only when the Indonesian state enshrined a degree of self-governance and recognition of Acehnese distinctive identity in its negotiated autonomy that Acehnese began to accept once again the broader Indonesian nation. In Papua, the conflict has remained at a stalemate and the Indonesian state continues to apply a variety of repressive and divisive tactics to quell nationalist demands.

The Philippines

State nationalism had a much weaker expression in the Philippines than in Indonesia or Thailand. The failed revolution arrested much of the nationalist, emancipatory thrust that the nascent movement might have developed and used as a unifying tool against colonial rulers, as it did in Indonesia. The United States colonial period also saw the establishment of new state institutions that survived after colonialism ended, and attenuated anti-colonial mobilization.

The Philippine state and constitution never enshrined nor even suggested a model of unitary state or emphasis on a single nation as was the case in Indonesia, Burma, or Thailand. Since its institutions and every constitution since 1935 reproduced a version of the liberal republicanism of the United States constitution, it conceptually aspired to combine liberal rights and representation, as well as regional representation through a bicameral Congress without recognizing ethnic or national differences. In theory, such a system – and particularly since the Philippines enjoyed the longest period of electoral democracy in Southeast Asia – should have been able to be most broadly inclusive and capable of managing conflict. Yet, with its progressive association with the Catholic majority and state policies and practices that marginalized Muslims, "Filipino" identity never took hold among Moro/Muslims and contributed to the rise of the MNLF and the MILF 's alternative, sub-state nationalism.

State leaders supported a political system and policies that assumed and enshrined the idea of a Filipino nation. It favored the Catholic majority that had come to feel more "Filipino" than Ilocano, Cebuano, or from another ethno-linguistic group. The attempt to elevate Tagalog to a national language of "Pilipino" is the most direct cultural policy that reflected state nationalism. But more significantly was the dominance of Catholicism at the heart of "Filipino" culture and state character. As Liow contends, already in the early 1920s, "the nascent Philippines state set about the talk of Philippinizing the Moros: altering local cultural and religious laws and commandeering land"

(Liow, 2016:66). The close symbiotic relationship between the Catholic Church and successive governments contributed as well.

Among Moros of Muslim Mindanao, an identity as "Filipino" not only failed to take root but became increasingly associated with majority repression. Aside from a shared religion, various Muslim groups in Mindanao and the Sulu archipelago had not seen themselves as part of a same community. But Moro nationalists, especially with the formation of the Moro National Liberation Front (MNLF), articulated a sense of Moro nation largely in response to decades of Muslim marginalization and exclusion, most concretely through lack of recognition of their norms and institutions that led to the state seizing land and distributing it to Christian migrants from Luzon and other parts of the archipelago. State policies of nation-building and their impact on Moros increasingly turned the latter against an association with a broader "Filipino" nation, which they saw as repressive (Liow, 2016:66–67; 77–79). The Philippine Armed Forces' operations against the MNLF, particularly under Marcos, strengthened sub-state nationalism.

The later breakaway Moro Islamic Liberation Front somewhat divided the Moro nationalist movement, with an emphasis on Islam being more strongly advocated while continuing to emphasize the common identity as Moro. Moreover, with the MILF rooted in the Maguindanao community and the MNLF stronger among the Tausug, the rivalry between both organizations sometimes pulled Moros in different directions: as sharing a common faith, belonging to a Moro nation, or divided among different ethnic communities with only superficial common bonds as Moro. Nevertheless, in recent years, the central concept of "Bangsamoro" re-emerged, which literally translates as "Moro nation." It revived and consolidated the nationalist appeal of a Moro nation, with the MILF sealing its leadership.

The failed revolution and establishment of a Commonwealth government under American colonial rule significantly diluted or even thwarted the rise of a nationalist movement. As James Putzel noted, "Since the stillborn birth of the first Philippine Republic in June 1898, the people of this repeatedly colonized archipelago have struggled to define what it means to be Filipino" (Putzel, 2000:170). While the nascent nationalist movement had roots in principles of equality with colonizers and unity of the archipelago, under the Propaganda Movement in the late 1870s to Jose Rizal's *Liga Filipina*, they failed to produce lasting principles or discourse that could survive the United States' crushing of the revolutionary expression of nationalism after 1898.

Instead, the US created an alliance with the wealthy land-owning elite, and progressively provided it with control over state institutions it crafted. American colonial administrative structures solidified the economic and political power of local ruling clans, dominated by landowners and their families. They integrated local leaders to the colonial structure and, later, the structures of elected political offices. From 1935 to 1946, the US relinquished much of the daily administration of the colony to a Commonwealth government. The US style parliamentary system that the colonial government crafted was constituted of both a House of Representatives and a Senate, both elected chambers with the latter representing regions in a parallel structure to the US Congress. Elections were also held at the municipal level. With the colonial government preventing the rise of ideologically based or strongly anti-colonial resistance movements, the political space was mostly occupied by existing landowning and locally based wealthy families that the American administration supported during the Commonwealth years. As a result, representation and power of the wealthy landowners ensured that they would preserve the political system (Anderson, 1988:10–15).

After independence in 1946, the Philippine state essentially perpetuated the established structure of the land-owning/political clan dominance that the American colonial authorities created and supported in the previous decade. Dominant families formed political clans that occupied municipal and provincial offices, as well as the bulk of representatives in Congress. While there is some debate as to whether the state was weak and porous, as if often portrayed in the literature, it is clear that a small elite blended its economic interests and those of the state. State resources supported those business interests, and allowed the land-owners to transform themselves into agro-business and industrial entrepreneurs, and mostly maintain their overall dominance of most economic and political sectors. There were few differences in the dominant political parties, or even the policies from one administration to the next (Bertrand, 2013:71–77, Sidel, 1999).

In this context, class divisions and rebellion became the main cleavage. The Hukbalahap rebellion (1946–1954) was mostly a communist-inspired peasant rebellion. With increasing and deeply ingrained inequality between the land-owning elite that controlled the vast majority of land and an impoverished landless peasantry, the rebellion in the countryside of Luzon was unsurprising. It failed but became one of several rebellions from the left that later supported the re-emergence of the Communist Party of the Philippines in the late 1960s and the growth in ranks of the New People's Army (NPA). The long-standing presence and mobilization from the left continues to represent much of the political resistance to the small elite that dominates the Philippine state and economy (Putzel, 1992, 1999).

Against this backdrop, the notion of Philippine state nationalism is necessarily filtered through this structure of dominance. There were few signs of ethno-linguistic divisions, and little imperative for the state to project strong cultural policies to enhance the Filipino nation. The ruling clans that alternated in power were more concerned with maintaining their grip over the state and using it to enhance their economic power. There were comparatively few overtly nationalist attempts to create state-driven projects to unify the country, as the elite oligarchy already controlled the political structures.

The promotion of "Pilipino" perhaps comes closest to policies in other countries designed to enhance the nation. During the Commonwealth years, President Quezon created the National Language institute which recommended that Tagalog be used as the basis of a national language. Yet, well into the 1960s, presidents and many members of parliament mostly used English in their public and official speeches. After 1959, the national language based on Tagalog was renamed "Pilipino," in an attempt to foster a more neutral label and national adherence to the single language (Tarling, 2004:172).

Moro resistance to the Philippine state was ambiguous prior to the 1970s. By some accounts, Moros successfully resisted Spanish colonial expansion and were therefore able to maintain their separate Muslim identity while the rest of the archipelago was not only occupied but also its people mostly converted to Christianity (Majul, 1973). They also resisted American occupation. By other revisionist accounts, as McKenna has argued, Moro leaders largely cooperated with American authorities who integrated them as officials within the newly established local positions, while preserving their traditional status as *datus*. He argues that there is little evidence even to suggest any large scale, and certainly not a pan-Muslim, alliance against the Spanish and therefore only weak sense of belonging to a common Moro group. Instead, while Moro datus became integrated to the new institutions, it was partly American policies of creating a Moro province that gave shape to a broader common identity (McKenna, 1998:82).

Ironically, Muslim identity was even nurtured under the American occupation as a way to co-opt Muslim elites into the state. As Abinales argues, Muslim identity was used to "keep Muslims "integrated in the larger Philippine body politic through the co-optation of "brokering" Muslim elites." These preserved identity differences "as part of the process of nation-building and state construction" in order to simultaneously reduce secessionist tendencies and provide access to the state for those Muslims deemed to be loyal (Abinales, 2000:3). This practice was perpetuated beyond the end of US colonial rule, and well into the 1960s. Consequently, resistance to the Philippine state is much more recent than simply the development of a Muslim identity and its difference from the Filipino majority (Abinales, 2000:4).

Two factors intensified the differentiation of Moros from the Filipino majority. First, while not by state design, the close association of Catholicism with

Filipino identity created a sense of Moro alienation. Second, policies during the Commonwealth years contributed to marginalizing and displacing Moros from their land. Repression particularly under the Marcos regime fueled the sub-state nationalist response.

Catholicism was entrenched already under the Spanish colonial system but it also informed the nationalist movement. At the eve of independence, Catholic and national identities were intertwined to the point that there was some consideration of making Catholicism the official religion of state. While this option was rejected, and the principle of separation of Church and state upheld, the Catholic Church nevertheless continued to play a significant informal political role, and Catholic identity permeated the Philippine state and nation. As Sapitula argues: "Catholicizing Filipino-ness emerged alongside the ongoing quest for national identity" and conflating both identities "allowed religious interests to exert influence on the fabric of nation-building" (Sapitula, 2020:52).

Equally significant, during the Commonwealth and early years after independence Moros were increasingly marginalized and displaced from their lands. Under the Regalian doctrine that gave the state ownership of untitled land, the Philippine state allocated land titles in Mindanao to a massive number of Filipinos from Luzon. The mass migration and land allocations displaced Moros, and made them a minority in Mindanao where they had previously been the majority occupants. The state ignored customary law among the Moros and considered the land unoccupied, as it had never granted official titles nor recognized Moro land rights. The Bureau of Lands made little effort to socialize Moros to the new regime and, instead, provided support and subsidies to migrating Christians (O'Shaughnessy, 1975:377).

These factors laid the foundation for the later emergence of a Moro sub-state nationalism. During the decades of Muslim elite co-optation, Muslims were largely quiescent as local elites expanded their socioeconomic power and occupied state positions. As in the rest of the Philippines, the system reproduced the power of these local "bosses" who controlled the economy and political institutions, and could use state resources to further enhance support with local patronage (Sidel, 1999:145–147). Expanding the franchise to Muslims, providing local elites with representation in the Philippine state, and using patronage to reward loyalty, the system could both recognize Muslim difference and ensure that they were increasingly absorbed into a Philippine state, if not a broader Filipino national identity (Abinales, 2000). But this elite co-optation disguised the marginalization that the majority of Muslims experienced, particularly as they were displaced through land acquisition.

The delicate balance of maintaining difference while fostering integration reached its limits under Ferdinand Marcos. By the 1960s, an alternative elite began to turn Muslim/Moro identity in opposition to the Philippine state and nation. The formation of the Muslim Independence Movement (MIM) in 1968 and then the Moro National Liberation Front in 1969 provided vehicles for articulating a new, sub-state nationalist resistance. From that time, the identity as Moro became much more widespread and defined as a nation in contrast and opposition to a Filipino identity.

The Marcos administration and martial law regime broke the previous understanding with local Muslim elites and intensified local grievances. Even before martial law, Marcos had attempted to centralize the state and weaken the power of local political bosses. Marcos implemented a new developmentalist agenda that saw state agencies interfere more regularly and expand resources in Mindanao. In the absence of vast personal wealth, Marcos sought to tap ever greater state resources. Development projects, increasing state control over resources, infrastructure and land, as well as manipulating elections to favour allies became more frequent. Mindanao was a rich frontier where the Marcos administration greatly increased its intervention. In doing so, it also became involved in power competition among political clans, and taking sides in local clashes between Muslim and Christian politicians in cities such as Cotabato city, where Muslims had lost their majority status. During the early Marcos years, vast numbers of migrants had continued to move to Mindanao in search of opportunities, given its land and rich resources. Marcos' development initiatives increased even more its attractiveness so that conflict between settlers and locals, particularly Muslims, became increasingly frequent. Since Muslims had gained little improvement in livelihood or opportunities, the resentment grew stronger, even against local Muslim elites who seemed incapable of countering the migratory flows and diverting development resources to the benefit of Muslim communities (Abinales, 2000:155–167).

The Moro National Liberation Front began to articulate most clearly a nationalist response to past grievances and their intensification under Marcos. Violent resistance had been on the rise in the 1960s, mostly against settlers, with MIM beginning to provide some leadership. But it was a rising intellectual élite, led by Nur Misuari, who gave an overtly nationalist direction to the resistance. The MNLF articulated most clearly the concept of a Moro nation to build unity among the diverse Muslim ethnic groups in Mindanao and the Sulu archipelago.

Armed resistance and demands for independence erupted in 1972. Against the backdrop of increasing tensions and violent clashes in previous years, the increased repression under the Marcos administration consolidated support for the MNLF's armed rebellion. In March 1968, the Philippe armed forces executed a group of Muslim military trainees in what became known as the Jabidah massacre. The event was a catalyst that allowed a new leadership to emerge and mobilize as the MIM. The MNLF also tapped into the outrage of Jabidah to recruit members and organize its insurgency. Marcos' declaration of martial law in 1972 provided further justification for the rebellion, and contributed to the MNLF's rapid ability to form a significantly strong rebel army. The MNLF demanded a withdrawal of troops from the Southern Philippines, more autonomy as well as Islamic law in Muslim areas. By 1974, it was asking for full independence and the formation of a Bangsamoro Republic. With more than 30,000 fighters by 1975, in only a few years the MNLF had achieved the ability to give clear direction to a new Moro nationalist movement (Molloy, 1988).

The steps toward such an alternative movement required a new leadership to emerge, but its foundations lied in the sustained differentiation and state policies that deepened Muslim grievances. Land displacement and lack of recognition of local Muslim customary land use greatly intensified with increased migration from other regions of the Philippines. In turn, these exacerbated poverty among Muslims and inequality. The ambiguity and claim to inclusiveness of a Filipino identity vanished as Muslims felt aggrieved from their socioeconomic loss, and the increasing presence of Christian migrants who were the main beneficiaries of state development policies. Furthermore, the Muslim elite's brokering role that had cushioned the differentiation between Christians and Muslims, and ensured some degree of inclusion within the state, was shattered with the increasingly clear marginalization. When repression rose and the state increased violence against Muslims, first in the symbolically key Jabidah massacre and then martial law, the final rupture was made. The MNLF could tap into this resentment to articulate its alternative nationalist vision, and more starkly denounce the Philippine state as colonizing Moros, and Filipino identity as being that of the Christian majority.

Nevertheless, the unity of purpose and overarching identity as Moro proved somewhat fragile. While the support for the MNLF and the struggle it led was high, it did not survive the Philippine state's successful strategy to weaken and undermine it through negotiation. After the MNLF reached the peak of its insurgency in 1974, the Marcos regime opened up negotiations under the Organisation of Islamic Cooperation's mediation. The Tripoli agreement of 1976 responded to many of the MNLF's demands, in particular granting autonomy to thirteen provinces and nine cities in Mindanao and the Sulu archipelago. The agreement failed as Marcos proceeded to organizing a plebiscite that led to the creation of two autonomous regions in a territory much smaller than the agreement had stipulated. Furthermore, Marcos had little intention of implementing most provisions of the agreement (McKenna, 1998:168). With offers of amnesty and incentives to lure MNLF combatants to abandon the struggle, however, Marcos succeeded in significantly weakening the organization. When the MNLF rejected the agreement on the basis of Marcos' approach and resumed its struggle, it had lost much of the support and strength it had previously enjoyed (Molloy, 1988).

The Tripoli agreement would remain a benchmark and a strong base for future negotiations despite the state's unwillingness to implement it. It clearly recognized the distinct character of the Moros, and also provided very significant territorial control as well as elements of self-government. But it was also an instrument of state manipulation to defuse the MNLF, and lacked genuine mechanisms for implementation.

The Moro/Muslim movement became divided with slightly different visions. In protest at the MNLF's agreement with the Marcos regime, and also Nur Misurari and the Tausug's dominance of the organization, Hashim Salamat left the MNLF and created a rival organization, the Moro Islamic Liberation Front (MILF). With a base among the Maguindanao people, the MILF showed the continued divide between different ethnic groups among Moros. At least for some time, the MNLF had achieved some degree of unity under the banner of a Moro nation, but ethnic divisions had centrifugal effects. While also appropriating the Moro nation as a core concept, the MILF used Islam to unify different groups. Islam was considered a more promising base of unity than the secularist nationalist appeal of the MNLF that was also neo-Marxist in its orientation. The MILF increasingly became the leader of the Moro movement, as it was best able to pursue armed struggle and negotiate more strongly with the Philippine state.

Early attempts at accommodating the Moros failed both on account of recognition of distinctiveness as well as significant territorial concessions. The 1987 constitution opened up recognition of distinctiveness by enshrining autonomy for the "Cordillera" and "Muslim Mindanao," without defining and elaborating on the basis for such recognition. While it created a supportive constitutional provision to push forward autonomy and recognition for Muslims, it also created sufficient ambiguity that preserved fundamental disagreement about its meaning and implications in future negotiations and legislation. The MNLF swiftly rejected the creation of the Autonomous Region of Muslim Mindanao (ARMM) shortly after the new constitution was adopted. It disagreed both on its territorial definition and the nature of the autonomy it created. The MNLF considered "Muslim Mindanao" to represent its historical homeland, which it had already given up part of through the 1976 Tripoli Agreement. The government of the Philippines considered that it meant a region where Muslims were a majority. While the MNLF accepted to govern the ARMM provisionally after it signed a peace agreement in 1996, it had neither accepted the state's conceptualization of Muslim Mindanao nor the governance structures that it controlled. Devoid of legitimacy or more effective institutional architecture, the ARMM mostly floundered and several MNLF leaders rejected it. Meanwhile, Congress debated several iterations of autonomy bills that were supposed to reflect the 1996 agreement, but each iteration was diluted and diverged considerably from it. A final bill "lapsed into law" when Gloria Macapagal-Arroyo decided not to sign it after it was passed in Congress. The constitutional provision allowed it to become law without President Macapagal-Arroyo needing to give it a formal stamp of approval. On political grounds, she was in a challenging position as the bill had lost support among Muslims, few of whom actually participated in its drafting, debate or passing (Bertrand, 2000, Bertrand, 2021:149–158, Magdalena, 1997, May, 1987).

The MILF considered previous agreements to have failed on several accounts. Most importantly, while the state had recognized Moros, their status as a sub-state nation remained vague and unclear. Furthermore, both territorial control and governance mechanisms failed to fully reflect Moros' quest for some degree of self-determination. Future negotiations would sharpen demands for explicit recognition of the Moro nation, as well as more credible guarantees of territorial control and effective institutions for self-government.

The MILF spent the following two decades continuing its armed insurgency, while negotiating with the Philippine state. While its military successes varied considerably, particularly after the Philippine military captured camp Abubakar, its main headquarters, it nevertheless maintained sufficient armed resistance to keep the state at the negotiating table. The negotiations waxed and waned from one administration to the next, but they progressed overall.

The MILF brought key concepts forward in its attempts to improve on the 1996 agreement. It insisted on a formal recognition of the Moro nation, Bangsamoro nationhood. It managed to have state negotiators accept its notion of a Bangsamoro Juridical Entity, which sought to give greater powers, autonomy, and an equal status to the Bangsamoro. The Supreme Court however struck down in 2008 an agreement between the Philippine state and the MILF on the basis that the BJE was unconstitutional, as it basically created a state within the Philippine state.

By 2012, negotiations finally reached an agreement, which became enshrined in the Bangsamoro Basic Law (BBL) of 2018. The BBL at a symbolic and substantive level enshrined recognition of a Moro nation, and gave significantly new powers and resources for self-governance. The use of "Bangsamoro," literally Moro nation, was a strong departure from the past and officially recognizes Moro nationhood. While this recognition might well be more symbolic than having real substantive implications, it nevertheless consolidated the Moros' status within the state of the Philippines with a formula that permits self-determination within existing borders. The BBL was a compromise that also enabled an agreement to be passed without the more difficult path of constitutional amendment. The MILF had pushed for the creation of a Bangsamoro Juridical Entity (BJE), which the government of the Philippines had accepted in negotiations but the Supreme Court in 2008 rejected it on the basis that it created a state within the Philippines in clear violation of the existing constitution and the integrity of the existing state. It took several more years of negotiation to produce a final agreement but the MILF accepted a lesser status within the Philippines in exchange for enhanced autonomy, clearer territorial recognition of ancestral domain and its Bangsamoro national status (Bertrand, 2021:162–174, Jubair, 1999, Liow, 2016).

In sum, while "Filipino" state nationalism was relatively weak, it nevertheless fueled Moros' sub-state nationalism by its association with the Catholic majority, state policies that continually marginalized Muslims, and by the intensification of repression under the Marcos regime. No revolutionary success nor strong nationalist state crafted, articulated, or attempted to design a Filipino nation. Yet, the core identity as Filipino failed to become a source of unity. Muslims were initially recognized and incorporated in the emerging democratic institutions, with elite Moros capturing local offices with American support and the broader Muslim population gaining both a right to vote, more inclusion in the state, as well as some occasional patronage benefits. But the majority of Muslims suffered not only from the perpetual inequality in a state dominated by wealthy landowning families and political clans, but also from displacement and marginalization as large number of Christian migrants were given land and state support across Mindanao. Combined with a rise of violence with settlers, and ultimately state repression from Marcos, the rupture with the Catholic majority and the idea of "Filipino" became ripe for national Moro leaders to nurture. Moro nationalists played a key role first in the secularist Moro nationalist discourse of the MNLF, followed by its more Islamist bent under the MILF. But the close association of the Philippine state and "Filipino" nation with Catholicism and the Christian majority, displacement, land seizure, state repression and violence crystallized grievances among Muslims and enabled the MNLF and MILF to channel them into an alternative sub-state nationalist movement. Although it was divided and sometimes significantly weakened, over the course of several decades the movement led to a recognition of a Bangsamoro and enshrinement of autonomy for the Moro nation in the BBL.

The creation of the new Bangsamoro autonomous region is an even more explicit accommodation of the idea of multiple nations within the Philippine state than accommodating Acehnese nationalism in Indonesia. In terms of adapting institutions to the distinctiveness of the group, its historical trajectories within the state, and flexibility to introduce an asymmetric arrangement, both cases are comparable. Whether recognizing explicitly as nations makes legal or substantive difference is somewhat secondary. Certainly, such recognition reduces the ability for the state to chip away at powers and resources that provide the tools for some degree of self-governance. Once recognized, Bangsamoro will have persistent claims to preserving their culture and distinctiveness with tools of statehood currently granted by the BBL. Aceh can more easily be reduced, over time, to an equal status of other provinces with perhaps a lesser claim of Acehnese to be different from other ethnic groups in Indonesia. But for the most part, the recognition is strongly symbolic rather than substantive per se, while making a significant difference in the group's members to re-identify on different terms with the state or the broader nation.

Myanmar

From the early days of its emergence, Burmese nationalism was steeped with ambiguity and ultimately failed to be inclusive. The anti-colonial movement was closely associated with the Bamar majority and Buddhism, as the outlier regions remained administratively separate from Ministerial Burma. With active engagement between leaders of Frontier Areas and Ministerial Burma beginning only at the eve of independence, there was little time for common bonds to form. As Anderson noted in the case of Indonesia, the interaction and engagement with one another of colonial administrators from various parts of the archipelago helped to create a sense of shared experience under colonial rule, which in turn contributed to imagining themselves as part of a common nation. Such common experiences were missing in Burma. While nationalist leader Aung San attempted to conceptualize a vision of Burma as being one nation that included ethnic minority groups, the recognition and institutionalization of ethnicity that followed ended up perpetuating and deepening divisions. Under decades of military rule, Burmese state nationalism adopted assimilationist and repressive policies that gave clear primacy to the Bamar majority, while only superficially giving recognition to "ethnic nationalities."[1]

---

[1] Ethnicity is a basic marker of identity and recognition in Myanmar, and has been associated with a number of rights, including citizenship, representation, and allocation of fiscal resources. There are groups of different sizes, and their political and legal status has varied over time. They are commonly referred to as "ethnic minorities" to distinguish them from the Bamar majority group. However, the umbrella term refers as much to large groups that have been provided with a state

In response ethnic nationalities developed alternative nationalist movements that have been strengthened over time.

Prior to the Second World War, Britain maintained mostly separate institutions for Bamar and ethnic minorities, despite some reforms. It introduced representative institutions in parts of Ministerial Burma, while much of the Frontier Areas were administered separately. At the same time, in Ministerial Burma, Karen, Chinese, Indians and Anglo-Burmans obtained some representation in parliament. In "Partially Excluded" areas, some ethnic minorities also could elect representatives. But, overall, these institutions did little to create a more unified population and remained, as Smith argued, "a curious patchwork of oddly different administrative islands" (Smith, 1999:43). Meanwhile, the British recruited among ethnic minorities, especially the Chin, Kachin and Karen for the colonial army and police, and only very few Bamar.

The rise of an anti-colonial movement was strongly Bamar-centric. The nucleus of the movement's leadership in the 1940s only had a few Shan representatives and few others aside from Bamar. During the war, the Burma Independence Army recruited mostly Bamar, with some Shan and Mon, to fight alongside the Japanese against the British. But most ethnic minorities remained loyal to the British and fought on the opposite side. Similarly, Aung San's Anti-Fascist People's Freedom League (AFPFL), although against the Japanese, remained overwhelmingly Bamar.

As the British agreed to negotiate with the AFPFL toward independence, the Panglong agreement created a new vision for a unified Burma. Aung San met in February 1947 with representatives from several ethnic minority groups, including the Shan, Kachin, and Chin. The agreement reached at Panglong aimed at including the Frontier Areas into a unified independent Burma. The main principle of inclusion was recognition of ethnic states and their inclusion within a federal state. The provisions of the Panglong agreement formed the basis of the 1947 constitution, which led to full independence in 1948.

Panglong held high symbolic value while the 1947 constitution enshrined ethnically-based principles of the new Burmese state, but neither constituted a vision of a unified Burmese nation. State institutions were created out of a political compromise, at a time when the British were pressured by decolonization in India to grant independence also to Burma. Enshrining ethnic states allowed Frontier Area groups to adhere but without the shared colonial or anti-colonial experience of the Bamar majority. The 1947 constitution was even

---

(such as the Karen or Chin), but also to many other groups that the government has recognized as part of its 135 "national races" *(taingyintha)*. At times ethnic nationalities and ethnic minorities are used intercheably. I refer to ethnic nationalities only in the context of groups that have developed a nationalist identity.

quite bold by granting several ethnic states the right to secede after ten years. Frontier Area groups perceived their inclusion as equals in a type of federal arrangement with rights to secession. From their perspective, the spirit of the Panglong agreement had been equality in a federal state (Silverstein, 1980:185–205, Smith, 1999:42–46; 78, Walton, 2008).

The implicit recognition of ethnic nationalities within a federal state clashed with a rising state nationalism focused on unity and a Bamar-centric Burmese nation. From the perspective of ethnic nationalities, a federated state under the Panglong agreement and the 1947 constitution reflected and helped to consolidate recognition of their distinct identities. But state nationalism in subsequent years sought to erode this recognition, and replace it with increasing assimilation. Using repressive means, the Burmese state implicitly and at times explicitly promoted state nationalism that reflected Bamar dominance, Bamar language and Buddhism. As a result, it contributed to consolidating and fueling sub-state nationalist alternatives that ethnic nationalities would espouse. During the following decades, these nationalisms expressed themselves through armed rebellion whereas the Burmese state attempted to implement a vision of a Burmese nation that reflected the Bamar majority (Walton, 2013). During the decade of semi-democratic rule from 2011 to 2021, negotiations were held but state policies continued to reflect strong dominance of the Bamar majority (Bertrand et al., 2022).

From the outset, the 1947 constitution contained a number of weaknesses. Most importantly, it failed to give equal status to some of the major ethnic groups. While it provided ethnic states to the Shan, Kachin, Karenni, and Karen, with a right to secede within ten years, it gave only a divisional status to the Chin, without the same powers as states, and no territorial recognition to the Mon and Rakhine, which the Burmese state considered to be part of the majority group since they resided in the valleys and had a long history of close relations with the Bamar. Furthermore, the constitution ambiguously recognized ethnic states but then gave strong, overarching powers to the Union government. The "Union of Burma" contradicted principles of federalism even though the constitution's details approximated those of a federal state.

The first government of the Union of Burma, under U Nu's leadership, adopted policies that very soon created resentment among ethnic groups. It already developed core elements of Burmese state nationalism that was built mostly around the dominant Bamar culture. First, the U Nu government made little space for ethnic minorities in the Union government and the armed forces were overwhelmingly Bamar. Second, the government imposed the Burmese language as compulsory language of administration and sole language of education after grade four. The Ministry of Culture and Education gave primacy to Bamar history and culture, and mostly disregarded that of ethnic minorities. Finally, through the Ministry of Religious Affairs and the Buddha Sasana Nuggaha organization, the government encouraged missions to the hill regions, where most ethnic groups had been converted to Christianity. The government centralized administrative and political power, and mostly bypassed ethnic minority states (Brown, 1994:34, Smith, 1999:79).

Within less than a decade, ethnic armed organizations emerged, claimed representation of their respective national group and rebelled against the state. Sub-state nationalisms consolidated as a direct response to increasing Burmese state nationalism. The Karen National Union was the first major armed group to oppose the Burmese state. It rejected the boundaries that were set for the Karen state and that limited the territory to areas where they were a majority, thereby leaving large areas where Karen resided but were excluded from the Karen state (Thawnghmung, 2011). The previous year, Mon, Rakhine, and Pa'O had already begun rebellions as they had been denied states. Initially, the Shan, Karenni and Kachin, which had made the most significant gains, remained quiescent. But the Shan began their rebellion in 1959 after a large influx of Burmese troops and central government officials moved to Shan state. They were joined by the Kachin in 1961, when it became clear that the autonomy provided to ethnic states was meaningless as the central government had continued its centralization policies and promoted mostly Bamar/Buddhist culture. When U Nu made Buddhism the official religion of state in 1961, he further contributed to alienating ethnic minority groups and associating the Union government with the Buddhist Bamar majority (Keenan, 2013:123).

General Ne Win's coup in 1962 only intensified tensions with ethnic insurgent groups. Initial peace talks designed to co-opt ethnic leaders quickly broke down. Other groups, such as the Chin in 1964, began their own rebellion. From 1962 to 1974 the regime launched intensive military attacks in ethnic areas, leading to massive displacement and destruction. Armed groups swiftly rejected its attempts to reach a peace agreement in 1963–1964 as it became clear that the regime sought to co-opt ethnic leaders without addressing their grievances.

The military tried to legitimize its regime and diversify its tools of political dominance with the adoption of a new constitution in 1974 and the creation of the Burmese Socialist Program Party. Under a one-party socialist state, there were no real powers given or concessions made to ethnic nationalities. More broadly the regime banned political parties, associations, and unions; it restricted freedom of association or expression; and it cut off relations to the outside world and expelled most foreigners, while it nationalized the economy. Overall, it increased centralization, repression, and the regime's ideological dominance.

Against the backdrop of the regime's new direction, apparent concessions to ethnic nationalities were merely cosmetic. The constitution restored ethnic states, while creating seven Bamar-dominated divisions. They could not organize political parties or civilian organizations to represent their respective groups. Governments of ethnic states were centrally appointed, and only implemented central government directives and policies. No powers or fiscal allocations were devolved to ethnic states or Bamar divisions.

Some relaxations were made to cultural and language policies but, overall, strongly assimilationist policies remained, which reflected the regime's Bamar centric state nationalism. The regime allowed ethnic minorities to promote their language and culture but with some limits. They could teach minority languages but only until second grade. Christian churches and Buddhist monasteries were allowed to teach minority languages after school. Nevertheless, Burmese remained the only language of government and education. The national curriculum promoted the history and culture of the dominant Bamar majority. Few ethnic minorities were given positions of power at any level of government or in the military's administration (Callahan, 2004, Callahan, 2003, Thawnghmung, 2011:143–150).

The end of Ne Win's rule and abolition of the BSPP changed little in these policies and, in fact, the military regime became even more assimilationist. The 1988 prodemocracy uprising against the Ne Win regime, followed by the dictator's resignation, elections and, eventually the crackdown in 1990 worsened rather than improved relations with ethnic minorities. During the brief period of opening after the demonstrations of 1988, leading up to the 1990 elections, ethnic minority groups formed new political parties and appeared to create a new common cause for a democratic Burma with the opposition National League for Democracy, and its leader Aung San Suu Kyi. But they had little time to forge a new alliance and jointly develop a renewed conception of nation or federalism for a democratic Burma as the regime failed to publish the election results, which exit polls had shown to be an overwhelming victory for the NLD. Instead, the regime cracked down on protesters, and banned the NLD and ethnic political parties. Ethnic armed groups continued their insurgency.

The military regime returned to stronger repression of ethnic minority cultures. It further restricted the teaching of ethnic minority languages and intensified its efforts at assimilation. As Mary Callahan noted, the regime's policies after 1990 were "the most concerted government effort at minority assimilation and disempowerment in the twentieth century" (Callahan, 2004:100).

Despite some minor changes along the way, Burmese state nationalism persistently failed to offer more inclusive and more accommodating policies to alleviate ethnic minority grievances and address their demands for an alternative conception of the Burmese state that could better accommodate their sub-state nationalism. Its shape and evolution continued to move away from the elusive idea of a Burmese federal state that would accommodate multiple nations, as some ethnic minority leaders saw in Aung San's initial nationalist vision and the Panglong agreement. The rise of ethnic armed groups, and persistent resistance to the Burmese state, continued to proclaim alternative nationalisms that aimed either for independence or a completely revamped notion of Burma/Myanmar around federal principles. The relatively mild centralizing and assimilationist tendencies of U Nu's democratic government already alienated ethnic minority groups. The more strongly assimilationist, repressive, and even more centralizing trends from Ne Win to the BSPP period, as well as the SLORC/SPDC military junta's rule deepened rather than reduced their grievances and fueled support for ethnic insurgencies (South, 2008).

When the military transitioned to quasi-civilian rule in 2011, new opportunities arose for reimagining and restructuring Myanmar to better include ethnic minority groups. The Thein Sein and USDP government began negotiations toward a ceasefire and a political dialogue that credibly changed the regime's discourse toward ethnic minorities. When Aung San Suu Kyi and the NLD won a solid majority in 2015, hopes were even higher that the democratic icon, who had allied with ethnic minority insurgents and parties in 1990, would push further negotiations and offer a new vision.

The initial stages were often symbolic but still departed from previous decades. First, the state relaxed restrictions on a whole set of organizations, allowing ethnic political parties to be formed, civil society organizations to advocate in favour of ethnic issues, and a dramatic expansion of rights of churches, monasteries, and other groups to teach minority languages and culture. Second, the civilian government opened up negotiations with ethnic armed groups, while allowing a vast amount of external funding to support the peace process. The terms of the negotiations toward a nationwide ceasefire and structure of representation in the political dialogue were largely designed by ethnic minority representatives. The formality of the process and ethnic minority involvement in the design stages were unprecedented. Third, the government created state parliaments, reformed ethnic state administrations, and expanded dramatically the representation and role of ethnic minority groups in state and local governments. It was implementing provisions of the 2008 constitution that was adopted prior to the 2011 opening. All of these changes constituted concrete steps to move away from repression and assimilation, toward giving greater meaning to ethnic states and addressing some of their past grievances (Bertrand et al., 2022).

Yet, the 2008 Constitution set the limits of expanding powers, representation, and additional resources for ethnic nationalities and did not represent a fundamentally different shift away from the state nationalist path set decades before. It did not enshrine any federal principles but retained instead the primacy of the Union, and the Union government. While new institutions were created at the state level and new powers defined, the Union government was given oversight and overriding capacities in every aspect of state governance, and retained powers to appoint Chief Ministers, the highest executive position. The Constitution and especially its appendices defined a number of different powers that were decentralized to the state level, which departed from the highly centralized structure of the past. Yet, at the same time, those powers were very specific and usually still under broader jurisdictions that remained under central government control. Furthermore, state governments' fiscal powers were very weak; so, in practice, the central government continued to hold strong control over all significant areas of state government expenses (Bertrand et al., 2022:55–60, Crouch, 2019). Finally, the Constitution explicitly referred to 135 "national races" (*taingyintha*) as a primary basis for membership within the community of Myanmar, thereby creating an ambiguous alternative to the states deemed to represent ethnic nationalities (Cheesman, 2017). Overall, the institutions did not enshrine representation for ethnic nationalities that would respond to their sub-state nationalism. Instead, they represented a slightly more decentralized form that continued to primarily uphold the principle of a Burmese nation within a largely centralized and unitary state. The recognition of 135 "national races" contributed to undermining sub-state nationalism and principles of federalism that the larger ethnic nationalities espoused.

In parallel to the expansion of representation and more flexible governance within the confines of the 2008 Constitution, the state and ethnic minority groups also negotiated toward a nationwide ceasefire and political dialogue to agree on changes to Myanmar's state structure. Launched soon after the inauguration of Thein Sein's civilian government, the negotiations promised a refreshing new approach to the conflict with ethnic minorities (Aung, 2016). While the overall achievements were more modest than hoped during Thein Sein and the USDP's administration between 2011 and 2015, nevertheless the state reached a nationwide ceasefire agreement (the NCA) that included a number of significantly strong groups, including the Karen National Union (KNU) and the Restoration Council of the Shan State (RCSS) as well as a number of smaller ones. While failing to convince many other significant groups to join, which remained unconvinced of the Burmese state's commitment to reform, the NCA nevertheless was unprecedented in its reach as well as its detailed, written provisions. As part of these, the USDP government also began the Union Peace Dialogue, which expanded representation to include ethnic minority representatives from several sectors of society beyond the armed groups (Bertrand et al., 2022:82–96).

The election of the NLD and formation of Aung San Suu Kyi's government once again raised hopes for a breakthrough that would create a new conceptual framework for Myanmar and enshrine multinational representation. Many critics and observers of the NCA and Union Peace Dialogue had attributed their modest achievement in bringing all armed groups into the fold, and meek substantive agreements, to high degrees of suspicion toward the military's continued dominance, its close association with the USDP administration, and a desire to prevent the USDP from capitalizing on peace to make electoral gains. The sweeping victory of the NLD gave much credence to skeptics and gave a resounding vote in favour of change. Ethnic nationalities hoped to see a new opportunity to reinvent Myanmar toward a fundamental restructuring that would meet their federalist aspirations. The Union Peace Conference was renamed with great fanfare as the Twenty-First Century Panglong Conference, in a symbolic recollection of Aung San's Panglong agreement with ethnic minorities.

Yet, few gains were made during the five-year dialogue. Aung Suu Kyi's government placed little emphasis on the peace process as it became increasingly absorbed by its objectives of reducing the military's role in the political sphere, and was limited by an apparent threat of crossing lines that would justify military intervention. While much blame for lack of progress can be placed on military representatives who dominated many of the Conference's committees, the NLD government nevertheless showed little leadership to push forward significant substantive issues in the peace dialogue and its policies continued to strengthen state centralization rather than signal a desire to move toward a more federalist model. By the end of its mandate, the NLD government had achieved little of significance in either new ceasefires or substantive agreements with ethnic minority groups, the Panglong Conference and the apparatus of peace negotiations was much weaker than in 2015. Several ethnic armed groups, in particular the KNU, had abandoned any hope that the NLD and the existing negotiations could lead to an agreement (Bertrand et al., 2022:96–109, Brenner, 2019).

After the February 2021 coup, all gains were lost. While the junta attempted to re-create some discussions with ethnic armed groups, they all returned to civil war and shunned any formal discussions. Instead, there were new hopes that the Bamar majority and ethnic minority groups could find common ground in resisting military rule. Many of the People's Defense Forces (PDFs) that were formed mostly among Bamar majority opponents to the regime sought refuge and even training in territories controlled by ethnic armed groups. At least in principle, the National Unity Government (NUG) that was formed from former NLD members as well as a broader representation from ethnic nationalities and other parties signalled a willingness to craft a new structure for Myanmar. Among ethnic nationalities, the NUG's adoption of Federal Democracy as its new concept for a post-coup Myanmar gave strong symbolic support and hope that a new threshold could be reached (South, 2021). Divisions and suspicions remained, however, and many ethnic armed groups began to doubt whether the NUG or a new civilian government under NLD leadership would deliver on promises made while in opposition. Meanwhile, Myanmar remained at war, the military strongly entrenched, and there was no apparent new direction that could reconcile long-standing divides between competing nationalisms.

From the outset, Burmese nationalism had ambiguous claims to inclusion, against the backdrop of early explicit recognition and territorial accommodation of ethnic nationalities. After independence, and most clearly during the decades of military rule, Burmese state nationalism combined periods of high assimila-tionist attempts, policies of ethnic minority exclusion, and high degrees of repression. The Panglong agreement and subsequent constitution of 1947 in theory created a state based on federal principles that could accommodate multiple nations. The lack of a broad-based anti-colonial nationalist movement had meant that ethnic groups from the Frontier Areas sought from the early days a de facto recognition as nations within a newly independent Burma, including rights for recognized ethnic states to secede from the Union. But Burmese leaders pushed further a version of state nationalism that gave primacy to the Bamar majority, Buddhism, and Burmese language. State policies continually prevented ethnic states from acquiring significant autonomy, and subsequent assimilationist policies eroded ethnic nationalities' cultures and language. The Ne Win and SLORC/SPDC regimes adopted strongly repressive policies during decades of civil war against ethnic armed groups, while also attempting strong assimilationist campaigns. The lack of significant accommodation along cul-tural or territorial lines, as well as the repressive and assimilationist tendencies of Burmese state nationalism contributed to the consolidation and perpetuation for several decades of sub-state nationalist movements from major ethnic groups. Karen, Kachin, Chin, Shan, Rakhine, Karenni, and Mon have all developed strong nationalist movements claiming more autonomy in their respective states under a renewed federal democracy. As Thant Mying U concludes: "The core strategy of the state since independence – of seeing Burma as a collection of peoples with the Burmese language and culture at the core – has failed, and will continue to fail"(Thant Myint, 2020:255). But the coup of 2021 pushed much further in the future any possibilities of crafting a renewed Burmese state that could accommodate multiple nations.

Thailand

Nationalism in Thailand developed differently from that in Indonesia as there was no anti-colonial, revolutionary movement that accompanied its rise. As mentioned previously, it corresponded closely to Anderson's "official nationalism" observed in declining European monarchies, which used new nationalist modular forms to reinvent themselves and preserve their rule. King Chulalongkorn's reforms in the late nineteenth century, accompanied by the strong emphasis on the Thai nation, was a similar defensive form of state nationalism that, although responding to colonial pressures in the region, did not have the emancipatory dimensions of Indonesian or Filipino early nationalist movements.

Thai state nationalism sought to downplay ethnic and regional differences, and uphold the unity of the Thai nation. While it was largely accepted among most groups in Thailand, it fueled a sub-state nationalist response among Muslims in the South, whose identity was more closely aligned with the Malays across the border. But it was its association with Buddhism and central Thai language and culture that made the "Thai" nation particularly alien to the Malay Muslims. Policies attempting to assimilate Muslims, marginalize their culture and Islam, as well as violent repression fueled an open sub-state nationalist movement in the 1970s that subsequently went underground. The revival in the last two decades of violent clashes in the provinces of the Deep South of Thailand is a symptom of continued impact of repressive Thai state nationalist policies. The absence of an openly sub-state nationalist movement in the last few decades was largely caused by the high degree of state repression but its existence and its political goals remain.

The 1932 military coup that removed absolute monarchy strengthened the state nationalist path that Chulalongkorn had begun. Successive constitutions beginning in 1932 changed political institutions quite radically over time but preserved the essence of the King as embodying the "Thai nation." Constitutional monarchy ensured that the king would play a key role in maintaining unity, protecting Buddhism, and strengthening "Thai-ness." Successive governments, under both military and democratic regimes, continued to implement policies aligned with this state nationalist project.

Early military rulers adopted strongly assimilationist policies. Phibun Songkhram's government in the 1930s and 1940s emphasized "Thaification." It issued regulations on language, dress, and religious practice that were designed to eliminate ethnic differences and promote a common Thai culture. These regulations were accompanied by Thai Buddhist officials, even in the Muslim south, enforcing these policies and reducing the previous tolerance of fuller expression of local cultures (Pitsuwan, 1985:61–69).

Many of these tendencies remained core to implementing Thainess, even though the most radical assimilationist policies were sometimes relaxed by some administrations. As Connors notes, the remarkable continuity of nationalist ideology after 1932 was reaffirmed at the first democratic uprisings in 1973, yet with democracy as an added element. When the Thai military returned to power in 1976, the National Security Council circulated documents designed to develop a national ideology to enhance Thai values and, in particular, its core aspects of nation, religion and monarchy. By 1980, the government re-established the National Identity Board (NIB), with a clear strategy to implement and reinforce Thainess (Connors, 2004:134–143). As Connors summed up: "The various activities that would emerge from the adoption of this policy included propagation of Thainess through the mass media, publications exhorting the beauty of Thainess and exploring the minutiae of Thainess (from the preparation of food to agricultural cultivation, architecture and beliefs). Through these efforts the diversity of people's lives were encompassed in the definition of Thainess" (Connors, 2004:145). The Thai state created a flag, a national colour, songs, dramas, novels, monuments and museums to shape and enhance loyalty to the nation (Thananithichot, 2011:256).

Throughout the 1980s and 1990s, the NIB continued a number of activities designed to spread and socialize its cultural propaganda. From programmes and magazines on Thai culture and art to the King's pronouncement there was a constant stream of propaganda to mould individuals into the state's conception of "Thai citizen." The NIB attempted to engineer the appropriate Thai citizen in a "self-reflexive manner in which the hegemonic project was mapped by the state" (Connors, 2004:159). While the campaign had little in common with the "decreed culture" of the Phibun era, and did not have the same element of compulsion, it was nevertheless constant and relentless. It went beyond defining cultural traits to also propagate proper moral values, citizenship qualities, and democratic Thai subjects. Even periods of contested democratic transition saw activists and regime opponents essentially adopt and legitimize democratic opening through Thainess, not against it (Connors, 2004:236–239).

The use of combined identities to identify local ethnic differences but reify their Thainess contributed to a kind of recognition of difference while reinforcing the common cultural and ideological sameness under the Thai nation. But it was often apparent that not all Thais were equal. As David Brown noted, Northeasterners were repeatedly discriminated against on the basis of their perceived "backwardness" and lack of sophistication, particularly when they migrated to Bangkok and were subjected to Central Thais' discrimination. Combined with the general poverty and inequality of the region as whole relative to Central Thailand, these local identity differences were reinforced by clear class distinctions. The education system as well as state propaganda sought to ensure that Thai-Lao would adopt Central Thai language and culture (Brown, 1994:82–84, Keyes, 1967). This form of "cultural imperialism," combined with regional inequality and poverty, laid the basis of an Isan-consciousness and resistance, and the emergence of a locally based difference of an Isan, or sometimes Lao, identity in opposition to Central Thai dominance (Brown, 1994:186). But while such consciousness and opposition translated in small forms of resistance in the 1960s and 1970s, its clearest manifestation, particularly during later periods of democracy from the late 1980s onwards was for Northeasterns to become a primary target for money politics, by which they sold their votes to politicians gaining their electoral support in exchange for short-term material gains. But they did not become a strong identity-based, resistance movement, as Brown notes, "[a]lthough the Central Thais recognized the Isan as a distinct community characterized by regional location, inferior status and a 'bush' dialect and culture, they saw Isan as referring intrinsically to a lower-status subgroup of the Thai people rather than a non-Thai category." In turn, although the Isan sought to "assert a distinction from the Central Thai ... Northeasters were inhibited from adopting an overly Lao-oriented identity" (Brown, 1994:203). Furthermore, it was easier to accept inclusion within a Thai identity given the relative closeness of various ethnic markers with Central Thai, with language remaining the most important distinction (Liu and Ricks, 2022). As a result, they would come to resist their socio-economic differences with other Thais but accept their inclusion as Thai-Lao.

Overall, though, Thai state nationalism was able to bring most Thais to accept and even espouse the state's propagation of Thainess. The popularity and reverence for King Bhumibol throughout most of his reign attest to the broad alignment with the monarchy and the values that it represented, even among peoples beyond the central Thais around which the cultural elements of Thainess were constructed. Where resistance occurred, it was often less a rejection of Thainess than an appeal for more space and recognition of local grievances and identities without rejecting the broader Thai nation. As Fong emphasizes: "the staying power of the Thai king is a function of material and symbolic culture that effectively harnessed historical, sacred and emotive capital of the Thai nation" (Fong, 2009:680). With an approach that was less directive and more propagandist, the state modified its campaigns to blend local identities with its ideal Thai citizenship model. "The monarchy has mastered the art of legitimizing royal rule by augmenting its overpowering and ineffable quality to maintain bonds within the nation" (Fong, 2009:678).

But Muslims of the Deep South, who retained their primary identity as Malay, developed an alternative sub-state nationalism in response, as they saw Thainess as Thai colonialism and repression. Malay Muslims are a relatively small group within Thailand, situated alongside the border with Malaysia. They are concentrated mostly in four provinces where they are a majority, namely Pattani, Yala, Narathiwat, and Songkhla. Prior to the territorial demarcation and consolidation of the Siamese state in the late nineteenth century, the area was under the control of small sultanates with very loose relations to the Siamese court. Already in 1832, however, the Thai state had obtained guarantees of non-interference under the Anglo-Siamese agreement that limited a British colonial role in these territories. After 1909, the Siamese state deepened its control by extending its administrative reach and replacing the local political leadership (Winichakul, 1994).

Despite their inclusion prior to the 1932 coup that marked the creation of the modern Thai state, Malay Muslims resisted inclusion within the Thai nation. Much of the resistance reflected grievances against the Thai state's increasing demands and administrative presence, particularly in raising taxes. Led by a former Patani leader, Abdul Kadir, a rebellion in 1922 successfully pressured the Thai state to ease some of its restrictions on Islam and to reduce the tax burden to align with that of the Malay population across the border. Nevertheless, this major rebellion became part of the history of resistance that an alternative Malay Muslim nationalism would use in subsequent decades (Pitsuwan, 1985:65–69).

A rebellion in 1947, known as the Haji Sulong rebellion, became a major historical moment of resistance that formed the basis of future narrative recollections of the rise of an alternative nationalist movement. Two elements came together and fueled the movement. First, the rise of anti-colonial Malay nationalism in Malaya inspired and partially influenced the rebellion. Second, the Thai state's adoption of increasingly assimilationist policies added to existing grievances. As mentioned before, the British proposal for a Malayan Union in 1946 sparked a new phase in the rise of Malay nationalism. The formation of UMNO in Malaya that year brought together dozens of Malay organizations and gave institutional direction to Malay nationalism. This movement spilled over to Patani, where local Malays had historically held close cultural and religious ties with Malays across Malaya.

But most importantly, against the backdrop of previous rebellion, the post-1932 regime and policies in the following decade created even stronger resentment. Although Phibun Songkhram's "Thaification" efforts targeted all ethnic minorities, they struck even harder among Malay Muslims. The Malay language was further sidelined and replaced for all official purposes with central Thai. In addition to the assimilationist approach to education and codification of attire and behaviour, the Thai state also encroached on religious practice, including Thai Buddhist officials overseeing religion. After Phibun's administration, there was slight relaxation of repressive policies with the adoption of the Patronage of Islam Act (1945). While allowing for some formal recognition of Islam and its religious leadership, the Act nevertheless attempted to reintegrate all Muslims under a category of Thai Islam and its concomitant administrative mold. Mosques, religious schools and *ulama* fell under the authority of the Ministry of Interior, through a top-down structure of state-managed Islamic committees. Haji Sulong, who was chair of the Patani Provincial Islamic Council, had become a spiritual leader for Malay Muslims and highly respected for his brokering role with the Thai state. But when the latter refused to negotiate on a proposed plan for an autonomous state, in 1947 he launched a rebellion. While it was crushed by the following year, it marked an important symbolic moment for Malay Muslim nationalism (Pitsuwan, 1985:105–108; 141–162).

The decade of the 1970s, when several insurgent groups rose in opposition to the Thai state, was the highest point of open expression and consolidation of sub-state nationalist mobilization. Field Marshall Sarit Thanarat's administration and that of his successor, Thanom Kittikachorn, had moved further away from an assimilationist approach to Malay Muslims by prioritizing instead development and education. Yet, the general thrust still reinforced greater integration of Malay Muslims and their institutions to the Thai nation and state. Religious *pondok* schools were provided with more funding, but were also regulated and required to adopt the Thai educational curriculum. While the reform program envisioned a more streamlined ability for Malay Muslim graduates to enter Thai universities, it came at the cost of abandoning the teaching of Malay in religious schools and increasingly teaching Thai values and morality based on Buddhism, as well as creating a new, loyal élite (Pitsuwan, 1985:188–208).

As a result, these accommodations did little to assuage Malay Muslim nationalists, for whom these measures amounted mostly to a different form of assimilation and forced integration to the Thai state. Several organizations formed in the 1950s and 1960s to resist the Thai state and propose a Malay Muslim nationalist alternative: the Barisan Nasional Pembebasan Patani (BNPP), Barisan Revolusi Nasional (BRN), Patani United Liberation Organization (PULO), and the Barisan Bersatu Mujahideen Patani (BBMP). The BRN, formed in 1963, and PULO, in 1968, were nationalist with the objective of obtaining an independent state. The BNPP, formed in 1959, had closer ties with Malaysia, and had its roots in the Haji Sulong rebellion, with a more irredentist goal of joining Malaysia. The BBMP was a splinter group from the BNPP and less significant. Overall, most of these groups organized sporadic attacks against government targets and used violence to promote nationalist goals. In the brief democratic period between 1973 and 1976, however, they used the more open political space for more peaceful resistance. The Patani United Liberation Organization was instrumental in mobilizing the religious leaders, students, and Malay Muslim officials making up thousands of protesters who demonstrated for forty-five consecutive days against the Thai state at the Pattani Central Mosque (Che Man, 1990:98–101).

From the 1980s onwards, there was little change in the Thai state's continued emphasis on Thainess, and the Malay Muslims' resistance to its brand of nationalism. While the main expression of Malay Muslim nationalism through insurgency essentially disappeared, it resurfaced several decades later in the form of smaller scale violent resistance. The ebb and flow of Thai state repression, both political and military, has varied somewhat with each administration, but overall there was clear evidence not only of continued Malay Muslim grievances against the Thai state but also of a rejection of its model of integration to the Thai nation.

A combination of repression against insurgents and greater development resources to the region contributed to reducing violence and assuaging some of the local grievances. Greater cooperation between the Thai state and Malaysia in the 1980s reduced insurgent groups' abilities to seek shelter and support from Malaysia, while the Thai state cracked down on the Communist Party of Malaysia, which had sought refuge along the Thai border (Carment, 1995). After losing external support, all insurgent groups basically disappeared or at least ceased their violent activities. Meanwhile, in an effort to eliminate future insurgency, a "New Hope" campaign offered amnesty to former PULO and other insurgent organizations. Furthermore, the Thai state created the Southern Border Provincial Administration Centre (SBPAC) in 1981 that, with patronage from the monarchy, delivered not only new investments into the local economy but also a brokering role that significantly improved relations between local communities and Thai officials. It aimed at convincing local Malays of the benefits of loyalty to the Thai state and nation. Particularly during the less repressive decade from the late 1980s and 1990s, SBPAC became the "front office" for the government in the South. It coordinated interventions from ministries, it maintained communications with the regional military commander and the prime minister and, most importantly, delivered programming that showed a slightly more flexible approach than previous assimilation attempts.

It funded some of the local pondok schools, and ensured that officials were more attentive to local customs and religious practices. It sponsored the creation of an Islamic University and increased funding for religious education. During this period the government even allowed some Malay to be taught in secondary schools and provided some support to attend the Haj. There was greater opening than ever before to Malay Muslims' religious identity and customs (Bertrand, 2021:211–217).

Yet, the reduction in violence and accompanying measures to improve local livelihoods were not sufficient to close the gap between nationalist visions. The Thai state remained firm in its centralized vision of the Thai nation, and its inclusive view of Muslims within that Thai concept. Its policies most clearly reflected these views. Despite some loosening in the education sector, it nevertheless maintained the centralized Thai educational curriculum and continued to support local religious schools only if they also adopted the Thai curriculum. It also continued to promote Thai values and goodwill from the monarchy, in particular as SBPAC remained under the close patronage of the King. Although mostly symbolic, the reinforcement of state ideology and symbolism signalled that accepting accommodation also meant becoming more Thai. Meanwhile, while the overall situation had improved, there was nevertheless a steady stream of violent incidents throughout this period of accommodation. At the very least these incidents suggested continued pockets of underground resistance to the Thai state, and sustained grievances. That most Malay Muslims saw relatively little improvement in their overall livelihoods and remained poorer than residents of other regions of Thailand likely fed much of this resentment.

As with repression in other cases, a sudden increase in repression under Thaksin Shinawatra's administration ended the apparently improving relations that had occurred in previous decades. Motivated mostly by his desire to reduce the significant political role of the monarchy, Thaksin's approach to managing escalating violence in the South backfired. By abolishing SBPAC, which was under the King's patronage, Thaksin essentially eliminated the one state institution in the South that had provided benefits and a bridge to the Thai state. Instead, Thaksin escalated the region's securitization by restructuring the security apparatus in the South, and providing the police with more exclusive management of the escalating violence while openly treating it as criminal acts, instead of reflecting any sensitivity to possible local grievances. As violence escalated and hit-and-run attacks on police and government offices increased, the police became more repressive. In 2004, two incidents gravely deepened resentment. In one incident, security forces stormed the Kru-ze mosque in search of militants, opened fire and killed thirty-two people inside the mosque. Later that year, soldiers arrested 1,300 peaceful protesters and piled up the prisoners in the back of trucks. Seventy-nine of them died of suffocation in what became known as the Tak Bai incident. Together these two events became symbolic hallmarks of Malay Muslim oppression at the hands of the Thai state, and became part of the narrative of victimization that encouraged stronger articulation of a Malay Muslim sub-state nationalist alternative (Bertrand, 2021:218–226, McCargo, 2008).

After 2004, there was virtually no change in the highly repressive approach of the Thai state and accompanying policies to integrate Malay Muslims to the Thai nation. For the most part, through years of protests, coups, and mostly return to military rule, the region was held under a high level of military occupation. The Thai armed forces maintained a disproportionately high level of troops in the region, while occasional violent incidents continued to occur nevertheless. The grievances remained high, and the Thai state basically offered a militarized alternative, rather than any significant gesture toward accommodating some of the long-standing grievances.

In recent years, there was a revival of some of the former militant groups, particularly the BRN and PULO. The Thai state agreed to recognize the BRN as the main representative of Malay Muslims in a first attempt at negotiations under Yingluck's administration in 2013. Negotiations ended with the military group that ousted her from power and were then revived when the junta agreed to negotiate with MARA Patani, an umbrella organization that was supposed to represent all insurgent groups. But negotiations again failed mainly because the BRN refused to join the broader organization (Bertrand, 2021:226–228). As it emerged as the strongest organization with military control of most militants in Patani, the BRN did agree in January 2020 to reopen talks when the military government of Prayuth Chan-ocha offered to do so at the initiative of Malaysia, which offered to play a mediating role. Nevertheless, as negotiations were held, violent incidents also continued to occur, and it remained unclear to what extent BRN was involved in these incidents.

The Thai state's concept of nation, deeply tied to the monarchy and Buddhism has remained alienating to Malay Muslims. They never supported the concept of becoming Thai Muslims, even though Muslim groups outside of the provinces of the Deep South accepted this identity, recognized themselves as part of a Thai whole, with some degree of difference on the basis of their religion. Instead, Malay Muslim experience at the hands of the Thai state went from assimilation and repression to small concessions on religion and language, but always against the backdrop of accepting a centralized Thai curriculum that reinforced central Thai culture, language, and values of the Thai nation, monarchy, Buddhism, and citizenship according to the state's view. As Liow also concurs, Malay Muslim sub-state nationalism is "further informed by the existence of an "other" in the form of an alien Buddhist-inspired nationalism imposed from Bangkok ... [and has been] a reaction not only to the centrality that ethnic Thai references and the Buddhist religion have assumed in ... Thai national identity ... but also the perception that these norms and values are being forced upon them" (Liow, 2016:133). In policy terms, where some degree of accommodation was made to improve relations between officials and local communities, or providing some developmental resources, these measures were aimed at gaining loyalty through improving livelihoods, but with little attention to the broader set of grievances around religion, customs, and language among Malay Muslims. This gap proved difficult to reconcile, and only widened after violent escalation from the late 1990s onwards. Repression and militarization not only failed to eliminate Malay Muslim grievances and demands, but also contributed to strengthening their sense of alienation from the Thai nation. Thai state nationalism, from its more assimilationist period to its slightly more accommodating phase, repeatedly fueled sub-state nationalism among the Malay Muslims.

Conclusion

In this Element, I have argued that state nationalism in Southeast Asia contributed to the rise or the intensification of alternative, sub-state nationalisms. While the origins and characteristic of nationalism differed significantly in Indonesia, the Philippines, Myanmar and Thailand, they converged in ways in which the state used nationalist policies, combined with assimilationist or repressive elements, to consolidate their rule. I have argued that two factors were key in stimulating or intensifying sub-state nationalist responses, in combination with some preconditions. First, the intensification of state policies designed to substantiate and define the nation, deepen its reach, and fashion loyal citizens created zones of exclusion among some groups. Second, when the state used repression and assimilation to further implement its state nationalist policies, groups oftentimes found new bonds and new mobilizational unity. Where groups were territorially concentrated, with significantly different cultural or historical differences, they developed their own nationalist aspirations, largely in response to these repressive or assimilationist policies.

Nationalism's spread in Southeast Asia galvanized anti-colonial movements and inspired states to tap into its imagery and unifying ethos to consolidate their newly acquired independence. Yet, it was layered over very different encounters with colonialism and types of political organization. At its outset, therefore, Southeast Asian cases show both unifying anti-colonial movements that nationalism inspired, such as in Indonesia and the Philippines, as well as "official" nationalism that Anderson associated with declining imperial realms, seeking to reinvent their basis of legitimacy and rule. Siam exemplifies the latter, when King Chulalongkorn began reforms under pressure from European colonialism and started to craft a modern "Thai" nation. While Indonesia and the Philippines were the proto-typical cases of constructed forms of nationalism, by which the nation grew out of former colonial boundaries with basically no cultural core, Thailand was a state-led attempt to use and redefine a cultural core to create an inclusive nation. Burma's nationalists tapped into the Bamar cultural core to build an anti-colonial movement but failed to define a broader and more inclusive national appeal when they suddenly needed to broker independence with ethnic minority groups. From the start, therefore, nationalism played a crucial role in transitions from colonial rule, with a variety of ways in which it enabled new communities to imagine themselves as nations, movements to unify against colonial rule through mobilizing particular cultural communities, or state transformation to tap into its power to foster new forms of political loyalty.

But after using nationalism as a unifying tool against colonial rule, nationalist turned state leaders then used it as a tool to consolidate their rule, and converged to a large extent in their approach. Whether tapping into the anti-colonial and sometimes revolutionary appeals that brought them to power, or through reshaping cultural traits, they sought to further define the character of their respective nation through a mix of cultural and educational policies, repression, and at times assimilation. States reshaped even the originally more inclusive nationalist forms in Indonesia and the Philippines. Policies designed to spread and deepen loyalty to the Indonesian or Filipino nation and state ended up narrowing their original broad appeal, through increasing association with culture cores and educational programs that reduced their appeal to groups such as the Acehnese, Papuans or Moros. Most significantly, repression and attempts to curtail local identities ended up fueling rather than eliminating the rise of sub-state nationalist alternatives. State-led attempts to create a broadly inclusive "Thai" nation similarly used a mix of cultural, educational, and repressive policies to instill "Thainess." In spite of attempts to broaden, the Thai state could not conceptualize and accept a Malay Muslim identity, leading to initiatives to accommodate them within the category of Thai-Muslims while applying strong repressive and assimilationist policies against the expression of a Malay-Muslim alternative. Despite adopting a constitution that recognized ethnic states and appeared on paper to accommodate ethnic minority groups, the newly independent Burmese state shaped its nationalist agenda through educational and cultural policies that revolved around a Bamar cultural core. After Ne Win's coup, assimilation and repression became its primary tool, which only intensified and entrenched the sub-state nationalist mobilization that ethnic minority groups developed in response.

There was nothing inevitable about the rise of sub-state nationalism among the Acehnese, Papuans, Moros, Malay Muslims, Karen, Kachin, and other ethnic minority groups turned nationalists in Myanmar. Other groups also felt marginalized, or oppressed, by states keen on defining their nations in terms that proffered inclusion while forcing different degrees of cultural, social, or identity shifts to "belong."

But in the same way that anti-colonial movements ultimately developed new claims to sovereignty and identities as nations independent and free from colonial rule, some groups under newly independent states would begin to claim a need for self-determination. That claim resulted from the limits of state nationalism's inclusiveness. When groups were exposed to repressive and assimilationist means of enlarging and enforcing the state's idea of nation, they felt unable to reconcile their group identities and experience with that broader vision. As Barter notes in this series, groups that developed secessionist agendas and engaged in civil war sometimes built on grievances from contested historical inclusion, but also from abuse and exclusion (Barter, 2020:23–24). Abuse and exclusion as I argue derive from state nationalism that set limits to the degree of inclusion and prompted groups to articulate a response also in nationalist terms, where the political goals became independence in the name of an alternative nation.

I have focused on this combination of state nationalist policies that, in becoming increasingly specific, tended to exclude groups at the margins. With a step further to repress and assimilate when met with resistance, they tipped some of them into shaping their own nationalist alternative. Sub-state nationalism was possible only where groups had the leaders that advanced and articulated sub-state nationalist goals, where groups could claim autonomy or self-determination in territories where they were sufficiently strong and concentrated. While leadership is essential to turn these sets of grievances into nationalist agendas, it only spreads and becomes a source of unity and mobilization when perceptions of exclusion and shared experience of repression have become widespread.

While state nationalism and its effects were relatively widespread, sub-state nationalist mobilization was mostly concentrated in the four countries and only among a particular set of groups. While one can count at least ten different sub-state nationalist groups in Myanmar alone, Indonesia had two, and the Philippines and Thailand one respectively. My claim is that sub-state nationalism arises in response to state nationalism that is insufficiently inclusive and implemented through repressive means. As argued, other factors were required in combination with these for such mobilization to arise and spread. The timing and sequence of articulating a more detailed state nationalism that became narrower, or the use of repression to implement it can be key. Much of the variance in the cases differentiated whether repression ended up being a source of sub-state nationalist mobilization or contributed to fueling it. Other nascent such nationalist alternatives, as mentioned above, failed to take root, mostly because leaders' claims did not resonate more broadly, as perceptions of state nationalism's exclusion is not always widespread. Repression is usually not applied broadly but against particular groups, which then provides the fuel that sometimes enables the articulation of sub-state nationalist goals to arise and spread.

Other groups might have felt excluded or been subjected to repression and assimilation in the implementation of state nationalism. Their lack of mobilization might be due to the absence of preconditions such as territorial concentration, leadership, and absence of shared colonial experience. But for the most part, a requirement was that state nationalism be sufficiently defined in exclusive terms, or be imposed. These factors were present in the more than fifteen groups covered in this Element. For others, such as Chinese in Malaysia, or Highland minorities in Vietnam, preconditions were absent. For groups such as several other regionally concentrated groups in Indonesia, most neither felt excluded by a more detailed articulation of Indonesian state nationalism, nor was repression therefore used to implement it. The same could be said for the Isan-Lao in Thailand.

Once articulated and mobilized, sub-state nationalism doesn't easily fade away. Nevertheless, two groups have been accommodated so far in Southeast Asia, leading to a reshaping of the Indonesian and Filipino state. In some respects, the originally broad and inclusive Indonesian and Filipino nationalist movements likely enabled the conceptual stretch to relax some of the more limiting state nationalist policies and allow an alternative expression of nationhood within their respective state boundaries.

Two important aspects of the institutional compromise, however, contributed most significantly to a settlement that could accommodate sub-state nationalist claims. Group recognition needed to go beyond simply recognizing cultural differences to provide at least some symbolic elevation of identity claims to nationhood, even if somewhat ambiguous. Enshrining the Bangsamoro label was a clear recognition of nationhood. Acehnese were more vaguely recognized as having a distinct historical identity and legitimate claim to some degree of self-determination beyond other ethnic groups in Indonesia. Most importantly, in both cases, self-governance with significant fiscal and administrative powers on their claimed territory sealed a compromise that allowed both groups to feel included on terms they could accept. Prior attempts to accommodate some form of group recognition or to provide elements of autonomous governance that fell short of credible control and autonomy over fiscal or administrative powers failed to resolve conflicts and led instead to greater suspicion. This is the case with Papua, which should have been more easy to accommodate along terms similar to Aceh. In the end, institutional flexibility allowed to accommodate deeply aggrieved groups that developed a strong sense of nationhood, without a significant threat to the existing broader nation.

One recent example shows how accommodation can help to prevent or defuse sub-state nationalist violence, but weak recognition and absence of significant self-governance can backfire. The rise of East Malaysian nationalism in Sabah and Sarawak has its origins in the failure of the Malaysia Agreement (MA63), which combined both territories with the Federation of Malaya. A new set of leaders have begun to articulate a sub-state nationalist alternative to what they perceive not only as the failure of the original Malaya Agreement but also the increasing perception that the evolution of state nationalism has increasingly excluded them. With its focus on Islam, Malaysia's state nationalism fails to be sufficiently inclusive for the quite diverse peoples of Sabah and Sarawak. While the original formulation of the Malayan Agreement provided recognition of their difference, by providing them with an equal status within the federation, some classic means of implicitly recognizing multiple nations within a state has become meaningless. For leaders of the rising MA63 nationalist movement, the Malaysia Agreement failed to deliver high degrees of autonomy or even significant control over local resources. Such accommodation also failed in cases of Aceh and Mindanao prior to more recent agreements, showing the need for both some form of institution that recognizes the distinctiveness of groups as well as significant forms of self-government. Moreover, in the East Malaysia case, the evolution of state nationalism is an essential component of explaining why the response is also in nationalist terms, with growing resentment from new nationalist leaders at the increasingly Islamic nature of state nationalism. What is still missing are significantly high degree of repression or attempts at assimilation that fueled sub-state nationalists in other parts of the region. While the movement in East Malaysia is still at its infancy, it certainly can spread and become deeper if the state begins to use repression (Chin, 2019, Chin, 2020).

By comparison, the deep-seated sub-state nationalist conflicts in Myanmar and Thailand show few signs of improvement, while their states have remained strongly committed to their core tenets of state nationalism and repressive approach to quelling alternatives. It would be a mistake to attribute failed attempts at compromise solely to the exclusionary forms of nationalism that developed in both cases. After all, they represented very different forms of failed inclusion. In the Thai case, state nationalism and articulation of

"Thainess" actually was meant to be broadly inclusive, but it suffered from a lack of broad mobilizational support from below and therefore reached its limits when it was too narrowly defined and then strongly enforced through repressive, and assimilationist means. In the Myanmar case, state institutions actually enshrined recognition of ethnic states, and therefore could conceivably have developed into a truly flexible federal form that could represent groups seeking some degree of self-determination. The original political compromise at Panglong was less a concession to sub-state nationalism than a practical building of state structures that reflected the lack of common political community between the previously separate colonial administrative areas of Bamar majority Lowlands and other ethnic groups in the Highlands. Sub-state nationalism of ethnic minority groups solidified in response to the intensification of a Bamar-centric state nationalism in the following decade, only exacerbated further through violent repression, strongly assimilationist policies, and perpetual civil war that the suspension of democracy and the beginning of the Ne Win regime created.

It is not inconceivable that the Thai and Myanmar states could develop similar forms of accommodation that were possible in Indonesia and the Philippines. As I argued, even in the latter cases, several iterations failed because they either did not sufficiently recognize groups or provide sufficient degrees of actual self-governance. The Thai state would need to extend both its ability to recognize the distinctiveness of the Malay Muslims from other "Thai Muslims," and potentially grant forms of autonomy that have never been explored in Thailand's relatively centralized state. Such adaptation might be conceivably difficult to imagine, given the lack of attempts to accommodate so far, but not necessarily contradictory to a broader conception of a "Thai" nation. Some piecemeal elements certainly have been extended through some educational and linguistic policies in the past. For Myanmar, failures to give significant meaning to the enshrinement of ethnic states could more easily be redressed. Unfortunately so far, recognizing ethnic nationalities while also recognizing broader ambiguous layers of ethnic identities retained past tensions even during the period of relative peace from 2011 to 2021. Furthermore, basic elements of a federal structure have been enshrined in various iterations of Myanmar's constitutions, but devoid of real and significant powers of self-governance in ethnic states. After the 2021 coup, the National Unity Consultative Council (NUCC)'s adoption of a new charter for a Federal Democratic Union of Myanmar provided a political framework that came closest to reinventing Myanmar to be more inclusive of self-determination struggles of the ethnic nationalities. It remains to be seen whether new compromises between Bamar opposition elites in exile and ethnic nationalities could lead to a reconceptualization of the federal state and an abandonment of state nationalism centered on the Bamar majority.

Whether or not states in Southeast Asia recognize groups as nations is probably secondary to the more important ability to recognize their group distinctiveness and justify asymmetrical arrangements. Certainly, giving some measure of recognition and loosening state nationalist policies, as seen in Aceh and Mindanao, is beginning to produce better more flexible outcomes in a region that requires more innovation and originality of institutional crafting to reflect its immense diversity. Modified state structures can give implicit or explicit recognition to sub-state nationalism, and can help to defuse its mobilization.

References

Abinales, P. N. 2000. *Making Mindanao: Cotabato and Davao in the formation of the Philippine nation-state*, Quezon City, Ateneo de Manila University Press.

Anderson, B. R. O. G. 1972. *Java in a time of revolution: Occupation and resistance, 1944–1946*, Ithaca, Cornell University Press.

Anderson, B. 1988. Cacique Democracy and the Philippines: Origins and Dreams. *New Left Review*, 169, 3–31.

Anderson, B. R. O. G. 1991. *Imagined communities: Reflections on the origin and spread of nationalism*, London, Verso.

Aspinall, E. 2020. *Islam and nation: Separatist rebellion in Aceh, Indonesia*, Stanford, Stanford University Press.

Aung, S. M. T. 2016. The politics of policymaking in transitional government: A case study of the ethnic peace process in Myanmar. In Cheesman, N. & Farrelly, N. (eds.) *Conflict in Myanmar: War, politics, religion*. ISEAS, 25–46.

Barter, S. J. 2020. *Fighting armed conflicts in Southeast Asia: Ethnicity and difference*. Cambridge, Cambridge University Press.

Bertrand, J. 2000. Peace and Conflict in the Southern Philippines: Why the 1996 Peace Agreement Is Fragile. *Pacific Affairs*, 73, 37–54.

Bertrand, J. 2004. *Nationalism and ethnic conflict in Indonesia*, Melbourne, Cambridge University Press.

Bertrand, J. 2013. *Political change in Southeast Asia*. Cambridge: Cambridge University Press.

Bertrand, J. 2021. *Democracy and nationalism in Southeast Asia: From secessionist mobilization to conflict resolution*. Cambridge, Cambridge University Press.

Bertrand, J., Pelletier, A. & Thawnghmung, A. M. 2022. *Winning by process: The state and neutralization of ethnic minorities in Myanmar*, Ithaca, Cornell University Press.

Boland, B. J. 1971. *The struggle of Islam in modern Indonesia*, The Hague, Nijhoff.

Bone, R. C. 1962. *The dynamics of the Western New Guinea (Irian Barat) problem*, Ithaca, Modern Indonesia Project, South-East Asia Program, Dept. of Far Eastern Studies.

Brenner, D. 2019. *Rebel politics: A political sociology of armed struggle in Myanmar's borderlands*, Ithaca, Cornell University Press.

Brown, D. 1994. *The State and ethnic politics in Southeast Asia*, London, Routledge.

Brubaker, R. 1996. *Nationalism reframed: Nationhood and the national question in the New Europe*, Cambridge; New York, Cambridge University Press.

Callahan, M. P. 2003. Language Policy in Modern Burma. In Brown, M. E. & Ganguly, S. (eds.) *Fighting words: Language policy and ethnic relations in Asia*. Cambridge, MA, MIT Press, 143–175.

Callahan, M. P. 2004. Making Myanmars: Language, Territory, and Belonging in Post-socialist Burma. In Migdal, J. S. (ed.) *Boundaries and belonging: States and societies in the struggle to shape identities and local practices*. Cambridge, Cambridge University Press, 99–120.

Carment, D. 1995. Managing Interstate Ethnic Tensions: The Thailand-Malaysia Experience. *Nationalism and Ethnic Politics*, 1, 1–22.

Chauvel, R., Bhakti, I. N. & East-West Center Washington. 2004. *The Papua conflict: Jakarta's perceptions and policies*. Washington, DC, East-West Center Washington.

Che Man, K. 1990. *Muslim separatism: The Moros of the Southern Philippines and the Malays of Southern Thailand*. Singapore, Oxford University Press.

Cheesman, N. 2017. How in Myanmar "National Races" Came to Surpass Citizenship and Exclude Rohingya. *Journal of Contemporary Asia*, 47, 461–483.

Chin, J. 2019. The 1963 Malaysia Agreement (MA63): Sabah and Sarawak and the Politics of Historical Grievances. In Lemiere, S. (ed.) *Minorities Matter: Malaysian Politics and People Volume III*. Singapore, ISEAS–Yusof Ishak Institute, 74–90.

Chin, J. 2020. Secession Calls Rising Up in East Malaysia. *Asia Times*. Accessed November 15, 2023. https://asiatimes.com/2020/10/east-malaysia-wrestles-with-colonial-legacy/.

Connors, M. K. 2004. *Democracy and national identity in Thailand*, Abingdon, Taylor & Francis.

Crouch, M. 2019. *The constitution of Myanmar: A contextual analysis*, Oxford, Hart.

Day, T. 2002. *Fluid iron: State formation in Southeast Asia*, Honolulu, University of Hawaii Press.

Dijk, C. V. 1981. *Rebellion under the banner of Islam: The Darul Islam in Indonesia*, The Hague, Martinus Nijhoff.

Drooglever, P. 2009. *An act of free choice: Decolonisation and the right to self-determination in West Papua*, London, One World.

Feith, H. 1962. *The decline of constitutional democracy in Indonesia. Published under the auspices of the Modern Indonesia Project, Southeast Asia Program, Cornell University*, Ithaca, Cornell University Press.

Fong, J. 2009. Sacred Nationalism: The Thai Monarchy and Primordial Nation Construction. *Journal of Contemporary Asia*, 39, 673–696.

Formichi, C. 2010. Pan-Islam and Religious Nationalism: The Case of Kartosuwiryo and Negara Islam Indonesia. *Indonesia*, 90, 125–146.

Formichi, C. 2012. *Islam and the making of the nation: Kartosuwiryo and political Islam in 20th-century Indonesia*, Leiden, KITLV Press.

Gellner, E. 1983. *Nations and nationalism*, Ithaca, Cornell University Press.

Greenfeld, L. 1992. *Nationalism: Five roads to modernity*, Cambridge, MA, Harvard University Press.

Harvey, B. S. 1977. *Permesta: Half a rebellion*, Ithaca, Cornell Modern Indonesia Project, Southeast Asia Program, Cornell University.

Hechter, M. 2000. *Containing nationalism*, Oxford, Oxford University Press.

Hutchinson, J. 2004. Myth against Myth: The Nation as Ethnic Overlay. *Nations and Nationalism*, 10, 109–123.

Jubair, S. 1999. *Bangsamoro, a nation under endless tyranny*, Kuala Lumpur, IQ Marin.

Kahin, A. 1985. *Regional dynamics of the Indonesian Revolution: Unity from diversity*, Honolulu, University of Hawaii Press.

Kahin, G. M. & Anderson, B. R. O. G. 2018. *Nationalism and revolution in Indonesia*, Ithaca, Cornell University Press.

Keenan, P. 2013. *By force of arms: Armed ethnic groups in Burma*, New Delhi, Vij Books India.

Kell, T. 1995. *The roots of Acehnese Rebellion, 1989–1992*, Ithaca, Cornell Modern Indonesia Project, Southeast Asia Program, Cornell University.

Keyes, C. F. 1967. *Isan: Regionalism in northeastern Thailand*, Ithaca, Southeast Asia Program, Dept. of Asian Studies, Cornell University.

Leifer, M. 2000. *Asian nationalism*, London, Routledge.

Lieberman, V. B. 2003. *Strange parallels: Southeast Asia in global context, c. 800–1830*, New York, Cambridge University Press.

Liow, J. C. 2016. *Religion and nationalism in Southeast Asia*, Cambridge, Cambridge University Press.

Liu, A. H. & Ricks, J. I. 2022. *Ethnicity and politics in Southeast Asia*, Cambridge, Cambridge University Press.

Magdalena, F. V. 1997. The peace process in Mindanao: Problems and prospects. *Southeast Asian Affairs*.

Majul, C. A. 1973. *Muslims in the Philippines*, Quezon, Asia Center.

Marx, A. W. 2003. *Faith in nation: Exclusionary origins of nationalism*, New York, Oxford University Press.

May, R. J. 1987. The Philippines under Aquino: A Perspective from Mindanao. *Journal, Institute of Muslim Minority Affairs*, 8, 345–355.

McCargo, D. 2008. *Tearing apart the land: Islam and legitimacy in Southern Thailand*, Ithaca, Cornell University Press.

McGibbon, R. 2004. Secessionist challenges in Aceh and Papua: Is special autonomy the solution?: East-West Center Washington.

McKenna, T. M. 1998. *Muslim rulers and rebels: Everyday politics and armed separatism in the Southern Philippines*, Berkeley, University of California Press.

Molloy, I. 1988. The Decline of the Moro National Liberation Front in the Southern Philippines. *Journal of Contemporary Asia*, 18, 59–76.

Morris, E. E. 1984. *Islam and politics in Aceh: A study of center-periphery relations in Indonesia*. Thesis (Ph.D.) – Cornell University, 1983, University Microfilms International.

O'Shaughnessy, T. J. 1975. How Many Muslims Has the Philippines? *Philippine studies*, 23, 375–382.

Osborne, R. 1985. *Indonesia's secret war: The guerilla struggle in Irian Jaya*, Sydney, Allen and Unwin.

Pemberton, J. 1994. *On the subject of "Java"*, Ithaca, Cornell University Press.

Pitsuwan, S. 1985. *Islam and Malay Nationalism: A Case Study of the Malay-Muslims of Southern Thailand*, Bangkok, Thai Khadi Research Institute, Thammasat University.

Putzel, J. 1992. *A captive land: The politics of Agrarian reform in the Philippines*, Philippines, Ateneo de Manila University Press.

Putzel, J. 1999. Survival of an Imperfect Democracy in the Philippines. *Democratization*, 6, 198–223.

Putzel, J. 2000. Social Capital and the Imagined Community: Democracy and Nationalism in the Philippines. In Leifer, M. (ed.) *Asian nationalism*. London, Routledge, 170–186.

Reid, A. 1979. *The blood of the people: Revolution and the end of traditional rule in northern Sumatra*, Kuala Lumpur, Oxford University Press.

Reid, A. 2010. *Imperial alchemy: Nationalism and political identity in Southeast Asia*, New York, Cambridge University Press.

Sapitula, M. V. J. 2020. Articulations of Religiously Motivated Nationalism within Philippine Catholicism: A Critical Assessment. In Shani, G. & Kibe, T. (eds.) *Religion and nationalism in Asia*. 1st ed., New York, Routledge.

Sidel, J. T. 1999. *Capital, coercion, and crime: Bossism in the Philippines*, Stanford, Stanford University Press.

Sidel, J. T. 2021. *Republicanism, communism, Islam: Cosmopolitan origins of revolution in Southeast Asia*, Ithaca, Cornell University Press.

Silverstein, J. 1980. *Burmese politics: The dilemma of national unity*, New Brunswick, Rutgers University Press.

Sjamsuddin, N. 1985. *The republican revolt: A study of the Acehnese rebellion*, Singapore, Institute of Southeast Asian Studies.

Smith, M. J. 1999. *Burma: Insurgency and the politics of ethnicity*, London, Zed Books, 2nd ed.

South, A. 2008. *Ethnic politics in Burma: States of conflict*, Abingdon, Routledge.

South, A. 2021. Towards "Emergent Federalism" in Post-coup Myanmar. *Contemporary Southeast Asia*, 43, 439–460.

Tarling, N. 2004. *Nationalism in Southeast Asia: If the people are with us*, Milton Park, Routledge.

Taylor, R. H. 2005. Do States Make Nations? The Politics of Identity in Myanmar Revisited. *South East Asia Research*, 13, 261–286.

Thananithichot, S. 2011. Understanding Thai Nationalism and Ethnic Identity. *Journal of Asian and African Studies (Leiden)*, 46, 250–263.

Thant Myint, U. 2020. *The hidden history of Burma: Race, capitalism, and the crisis of democracy in the 21st century*, New York, W. W. Norton.

Thawnghmung, A. M. 2011. *The "other" Karen in Myanmar: Ethnic minorities and the struggle without arms*, Lanham, Lexington Books.

Vu, T. 2013. Southeast Asia's New Nationalism: Causes and Significance. *Trans-regional and -National Studies of Southeast Asia*, 1, 259–279.

Walton, M. J. 2008. Ethnicity, Conflict, and History in Burma: The Myths of Panglong. *Asian Survey*, 48, 889–910.

Walton, M. J. 2013. The "Wages of Burman-ness:" Ethnicity and Burman Privilege in Contemporary Myanmar. *Journal of Contemporary Asia*, 43, 1–27.

Winichakul, T. 1994. *Siam mapped: A history of the geo-body of a nation*. Honolulu, University of Hawaii Press.

Winichakul, T. 2008. Nationalism and the Radical Intelligentsia in Thailand. *Third World Quarterly*, 29, 575–591.

Cambridge Elements ≡

Politics and Society in Southeast Asia

Edward Aspinall

Australian National University

Edward Aspinall is a professor of politics at the Coral Bell School of Asia-Pacific Affairs, Australian National University. A specialist of Southeast Asia, especially Indonesia, much of his research has focused on democratisation, ethnic politics and civil society in Indonesia and, most recently, clientelism across Southeast Asia.

Meredith L. Weiss

University at Albany, SUNY

Meredith L. Weiss is Professor of Political Science at the University at Albany, SUNY. Her research addresses political mobilization and contention, the politics of identity and development, and electoral politics in Southeast Asia, with particular focus on Malaysia and Singapore.

About the Series

The Elements series Politics and Society in Southeast Asia includes both country-specific and thematic studies on one of the world's most dynamic regions. Each title, written by a leading scholar of that country or theme, combines a succinct, comprehensive, up-to-date overview of debates in the scholarly literature with original analysis and a clear argument.

Cambridge Elements $\equiv$

Politics and Society in Southeast Asia

Printed in the United States
by Baker & Taylor Publisher Services